CHAMBERLAIN AT PETERSBURG:

THE CHARGE AT FORT HELL JUNE 18, 1864

by Diane Monroe Smith

Maps by Robert E. (Ned) Smith

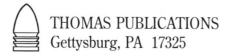

THOMAS PUBLICATIONS
Gettysburg, PA 17325

Copyright © 2004 Diane M. Smith

Printed and bound in the United States of America

Published by THOMAS PUBLICATIONS
        P.O. Box 3031
        Gettysburg, Pa. 17325

All rights reserved. No part of this book may be used or reproduced without written permission of the author and the publisher, except in the case of brief quotations embodied in critical essays and reviews.

ISBN-1-57747-098-2

The cover illustration, a pencil sketch of
Joshua L. Chamberlain, is by R. A. Taylor.

Dedicated to my father,
U.S. Coast Guard Machinist Mate Ralph N. Monroe,
and his shipmates on the
Destroyer Escort U.S.S. Ramsden, which carried them
through the Atlantic and Pacific Theaters of WWII.

CONTENTS

PREFACE

Considering the accomplishments and renown of Joshua Chamberlain, both as soldier and author, it is fortuitous when one of his manuscripts is found. Forgotten and unpublished, "The Charge at Fort Hell" recounts Chamberlain's experiences on June 17 and 18, 1864, at the Battle of Petersburg. Although Chamberlain wrote a speech that touched on this subject, which has been published, this unpublished work is a highly personal and less formal account of the days which proved so fateful for the new 1st Brigade commander. And while so much has been written about Chamberlain at Gettysburg, his story at the Battle of Petersburg is one that could be said to rival that of Little Round Top in the challenges it presented to the young commander.

The original manuscript is quite obviously a first or early draft upon which Chamberlain was working in 1899. It is typewritten with a number of corrections having been made in Chamberlain's handwriting. So, while we may not have this famous raconteur's usual polish, we are treated to the raw material of his thoughts. We can also appreciate to some extent the process by which he laid down passages that are among the most appreciated and best known of the many offered to us by Civil War writers. And there is a spontaneity and freshness about "The Charge at Fort Hell" that make us feel as if we are settling in an armchair opposite the aging warrior, and hearing him share his most vivid remembrances of those days at Petersburg.

While Chamberlain's handwritten compositions were monuments to correct grammar and spelling, this and others of his typewritten manuscripts have many typographical errors, many of which were so obvious that they were easily corrected. At the time "The Charge at Fort Hell" was written, it is not known whether Chamberlain was working with a secretary, as he would in the future, or whether he tried to master the typewriter himself. There are also occasions in the work where the intended meaning is clear, but a word or two has been left out. These have been added but set apart by brackets. In several cases, where Chamberlain did not know, or perhaps did not wish to identify certain parties, brackets are also used. Several sentences or phrases were crossed out and have been omitted from this work, though those of interest or which address any controversy are included in the endnotes.

Upon deciding that "The Charge at Fort Hell" should be made available to students of Chamberlain and Civil War readers, it occurred to me that it would be worthwhile also to shed a good deal more light upon Chamberlain's and the 5th Corps' service during General Ulysses S. Grant's

Overland Campaign of 1864. Though little that could be called comprehensive has been written about this period, there were important and startling events that are well worth telling. Therefore, "The Charge at Fort Hell" is prefaced by an examination of Chamberlain's and the 5th Corps' experiences in the spring of 1864. A thorough search for contemporary accounts and material was made for this purpose and to provide a detailed annotation of this Petersburg account. The material found for 1864 was so plentiful and thought-provoking, that it has provided inspiration for yet another book that is already underway. The conflicts that developed among the commanders of the Union army during the Overland Campaign and beyond had broad repercussions on the conduct of the war, and tragic results for the soldiers of the Army of the Potomac.

My special appreciation to William W. Erwin, Jr., formerly Senior Reference Librarian at Duke University Special Archives, for bringing the existance of Chamberlain's "Charge at Fort Hell" to my attention. Many thanks to Bill Matter for sharing his expertise, and for his kind advice and assistance. Special appreciation also to John McNulty, for his friendship and support. The Bangor Public Library staff, once again, provided invaluable research assistance and material. Thank you to Chris Calkins at Petersburg Battlefield for information he provided. Fred Bassett at the New York State Library made valuable research material accessible. Rita Bailey of the Pejebscot Historical Society helped me with a transcription of a letter which has gone missing from the holding institution. Thank you to Pela Rosenquist and George Pickering of Pejebscot for their much valued friendship, moral support and enthusiasm. Amy Rupert of Rensselaer Polytechnic Institute Special Archives, for her 'beyond the call of duty' assistance. I also wish to express my sincere gratitude to all the many scholars whose works are cited in this book. On the firm foundation of their hard work, this work was begun. A special thank you to the staff at Thomas Publications. I am most grateful to my husband, Ned, for all his support and encouragement, and for the superb research and work he has done in creating the maps for *Chamberlian at Petersburg*.

There was a wealth of material to consider, and I wish to point out that based upon this experience and that of doing research for a Chamberlain biography *Fanny and Joshua*, I found Joshua Chamberlain to be a careful and honest historian, whose accounts were frequently corroborated by his soldiers and fellow officers. Lastly, an appendix of relevant documents has also been added. I hope that this, the annotation, maps, and photographs that have been gathered here, will in some small way enhance the pleasure of reading "The Charge at Fort Hell."

INTRODUCTION

In the first days of Grant's spring campaign of 1864, the 20th Maine Regiment of the 3rd Brigade, 1st Division, 5th Corps, Army of the Potomac, marched without its colonel, Joshua Lawrence Chamberlain. As early as October 1, 1863, Chamberlain was clearly suffering with the symptoms of malaria that would soon take him away from his 3rd Brigade command. After Chamberlain did reconnaissance for a sharp fight at Rappahannock Station on November 9, 1863, his illness became critical when he slept unprotected, without fire or shelter, in a heavy snow storm. On November 15, Chamberlain signed a request for sick leave, his signature all but unrecognizable, and by the time he was sent to Washington, D.C., in a cattle car, he was unconscious. The diagnosis was typho-malarial fever. After a month at the Georgetown Seminary Hospital and weeks of recuperation at home, he was deemed strong enough in February 1864 for detached service in Washington, D.C., and Trenton, New Jersey, serving on court-martial.[1]

When Grant was appointed general-in-chief of the armies and the opening of the spring campaign was imminent, though Chamberlain was still suffering from malarial symptoms, he began requesting release from court-martial duty. While Chamberlain waited for release, in early April, General Joseph J. Bartlett, formerly of the 6th Corps, was given command of Chamberlain's 3rd Brigade in General Charles Griffin's 1st Division. This appointment sent Chamberlain back to command of his Maine regiment. Finally receiving orders on May 10 which allowed him to return to the field, Chamberlain left Washington, D.C., while it was in a state of celebration. Oblivious to the bloody stalemate at the Wilderness, many had embraced Grant's statement, "I propose to fight it out on this line, if it takes all summer," with optimism that the war in the East would soon be over. A number of congressmen stayed on beyond their session to be in town at the end of the war. President Abraham Lincoln, dismayed at the premature festivities, told a friend, "I shall be happy if we are over with the fight in Virginia within a year." The Adjutant General's Report states that losses for the Army of the Potomac and General Ambrose Burnside's 9th Corps at the Wilderness, May 5-7, 1864, were 17,666 officers and men killed, wounded, and missing. Aggregate 5th Corps' losses are listed as 5,132, but there is testimony that the 5th Corps' losses were considerably higher.[2]

By the time Chamberlain returned to the Army of the Potomac, its soldiers had fought the hellish Battle of the Wilderness but were still en-

NARA

Lt. Gen. Ulysses S. Grant

during the bloodletting at Spotsylvania. He returned in time to be given a special command of eight 1st Division Regiments, leading them through the dark night of May 17-18 toward the enemy line. The advance was made to secure new ground for the twenty-six 5th Corps' guns that would hammer the Rebel fortifications before another futile attack by the 2nd and 6th Corps on the morning of May 18, 1864. That morning, Chamberlain had command of the 3rd Brigade, as he would sporadically in the days to come, due to Bartlett's frequent illness. It did not take Chamberlain long to realize what the first two weeks of campaigning had done to this brigade. As with so many other brigades in the Army of the Potomac, it had experienced a staggering loss of irreplaceable veteran officers and men.[3]

Stymied at Spotsylvania as he had been at the Wilderness, Grant again turned from frontal assault to maneuver. In an effort to draw the enemy out of its fortifications, Grant directed the army to begin its movement on the night of May 19. A probe by the enemy on the Army of the Potomac's right was checked, but delayed Federal movement until May 20. General Winfield Scott Hancock's 2nd Corps moved before midnight for the Mattaponi River, aiming to place itself across General Robert E. Lee's line of communication. At 10 a.m. on May 21, the 5th Corps successfully extricated itself in broad daylight from its position in front of the enemy's fortifications. Though the Rebels shelled them and sent a heavy picket line after them, a well positioned 6th Corps reserve sent the Rebels back to their lines. But all, apparently, was not well.

Upon Grant's receiving word that Lee was responding more quickly than expected to Federal movement, General Gouverneur Warren's route was abruptly changed to one that would bring the 5th Corps closer to Hancock's position. The 5th Corps marched by way of Massaponax Church and Guiney's, but when bivouacked at dark near Catlett's was still fifteen to twenty miles away from the 2nd Corps. In response to Grant's movement, Lee had set his army into motion on a route which narrowly avoided an engagement with elements of the strung out Union troops. Refusing the bait of the isolated Army of the Potomac corps, designed to lure him into open field battle, Lee instead would eventually take up a position on the North Anna River, imposing the Army of Northern Virginia between the Federals and the vital Virginia Central Railroad and Hanover Junction. This was the conduit through which the harvests of the Shenandoah Valley passed to Richmond. By midnight of May 21, the last of the antagonists were abandoning Spotsylvania, the bloody field having claimed more than 18,000 Union officers and men killed, wounded, or missing. Since crossing

NARA

Gen. Gouveneur K. Warren

the Rapidan, 36,000 Federal soldiers had become casualties. Rebel losses at Spotsylvania were between 9,000 and 10,000, bringing total Confederate losses to approximately 18,000 since the beginning of the campaign.[4]

In the days after the Federal withdrawal from Spotsylvania, as Grant admitted in his memoirs, they "...had neither guides nor maps to tell us where the roads were, or where they led to. Engineer and staff officers were put to dangerous duty...." And, having allowed General Philip Sheridan to leave with the main body of the Army of the Potomac's cavalry on a raid, Grant was moving most of his infantry blindly through this maze. Lee did not labor under such hardships. Not only did he have men who knew the region well, but his cavalry and signalmen kept him fully informed of Federal advances. While Confederate cavalry commanders Generals J.E.B. Stuart and Fitzhugh Lee had pursued Sheridan, Lee had retained Generals Wade Hampton's and "Rooney" Lee's horsemen. Hancock had also unexpectedly met infantry resistance, provided by the first elements of General George Pickett's Division on its way to reinforce Lee. Meanwhile, a detach-

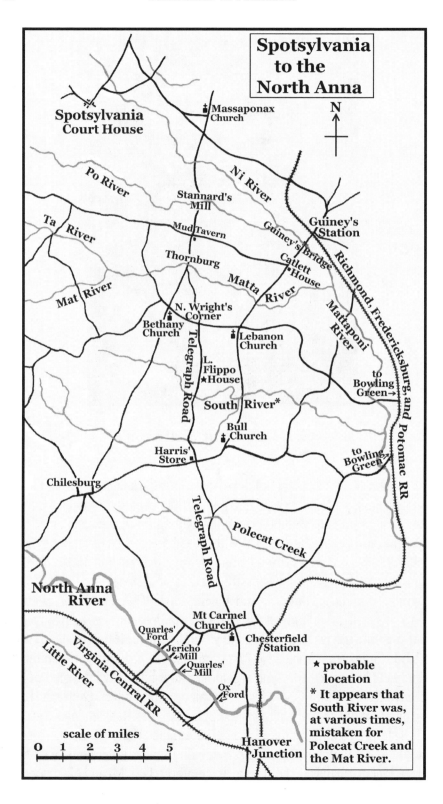

ment of cavalry under General Alfred Torbert that had accompanied the 2nd Corps had been bedeviled and delayed by Rebel horsemen. Though Hancock, on the afternoon of May 21, was able to consolidate the 2nd Corps in a position of considerable strength on the Mattaponi River, less than twenty-four hours into Grant's movement away from Spotsylvania, his plan to entrap the Army of Northern Virginia seemed to be disintegrating.[5]

NARA

Gens. Philip Sheridan, James H. Wilson, and Alfred Torbert, 1864

The 5th Corps' infantry outposts encountered only enemy cavalry during the night of May 21-22. But the picture of enemy activity became more clear when Captain Washington Roebling of Warren's staff went out before dawn on May 22 to Lt. Col. Edmund Mann Pope's cavalry vedettes at Lebanon Church. There he discovered that the cavalrymen had heard wagons rumbling south on the Telegraph Road all night long without reporting it. At 5:30 a.m., Roebling sent word back to Army of the Potomac headquarters that it looked as if Lee was retreating, and Roebling urged Pope to attack the last elements of the seemingly unguarded enemy train, but he refused. J. Michael Miller, in his *The North Anna Campaign*, seems to imply that 5th Corps infantry stood idly by while Rebel stragglers disappeared southward, but it

Rensselaer Polytechnic Institute Library Special Collections

Washington Roebling

appears that only the Federal cavalry had a real opportunity to strike at the Confederates. Roebling commented on the cavalry's failure to take up pursuit, "Here was a chance to capture the whole of Lee's wagon train; never was the want of Cavalry more painfully felt. Such opportunities are only presented once in a campaign and should not be lost."

Pope, of Penfield, New York, was the cavalry detachment's commander and acting assistant inspector general of Brig. Gen. George A. Custer's 8th New York Cavalry. Pope had been captured on July 10, 1863, and was later exchanged. He did not rejoin the army until May 12, 1864, too late to rejoin Custer, who was with Sheridan's expedition. By 1865, Pope would become a brevet brigadier general of volunteers.[6]

Change was the one constant as far as headquarters' orders for the 5th Corps for May 21 and 22 were concerned. Warren's orders for his marching route that he received on the morning of May 21 were changed before he moved, and the whole purpose of the Army of the Potomac's movement, to draw out Lee's army, gradually changed from one with offensive purposes to that of taking up defensive positions. Grant's orders to Burnside gave him some discretion should he meet with enemy resistance, and the 9th Corps commander, though the number of Rebels he encountered was minimal, took full advantage to change his marching route. Grant and General George Meade would learn that Burnside, who was to have followed and supported Warren, had not moved as expected. The arrival of news at army headquarters that some part of the Army of Northern Virginia had passed down the nearby Telegraph Road during the night of May 21-22 prompted orders that would draw the 5th, 6th, and 9th Corps together for pursuit of Lee southward. Further, it is not known how long it took for an erroneous report from Hancock on the morning of May 22 to travel to Army of the Potomac headquarters. The report stated that an enemy line of battle was approaching his position, but it had to be corrected when it was discovered that the "enemy" was some of the 2nd Corps' own men. Since the 5th Corps was relying on outdated maps that contained much false information, on May 22, detachments were sent out before dawn to feel for the enemy's position. Warren was also forced to launch a search for river crossings through a landscape crisscrossed with deep, unbridged drainage ditches. And, though elements of the 5th Corps had been ready to move at dawn, Grant had grown cautious, and Warren was instructed to await the approach of the 6th Corps.

At 10 a.m., just thirty minutes after the advance of the hard-marched 6th Corps approached Warren's position, the 5th Corps moved toward the Telegraph Road. By this time, the head of Lee's column was already on the North Anna River, where his numbers were swelled by General John Breckinridge's Division. Having soundly defeated General Franz Sigel in the Shenandoah Valley, Breckinridge was free to bring his 3,200-man division to reinforce Lee, and he was halted to occupy Hanover Junction. Between Lee's army and the Army of the Potomac, Hampton's and Lee's Cavalry Divisions, screening the last elements of the Army of Northern Virginia column, harassed and delayed the Federals.[7]

The 5th Corps was soon pressing against the cavalry that was acting as rear guard for General Richard Anderson's [formerly General James Longstreet's] Corps. With Bartlett again on the sick list, Chamberlain was in command of the 3rd Brigade. It was moving in advance of the 5th Corps column with a few skirmishers and scouts, "anxiously examining every point of advantage from which the enemy might turn upon us, and holding the brigade well in hand for anything that might happen." At midday, Chamberlain approached the South River, which the Federals mistook for Pole

Cat Creek. Near the Littleton Flippo House, Confederate Brig. Gen. John R. Chambliss' Cavalry Brigade, supported by two guns of Maj. James Breathed's Horse Artillery, was found deployed in the road ahead. Chamberlain, commanding the 20th Maine, 1st Michigan, and the 118th Pennsylvania, received Griffin's permission to attempt a flanking movement through the woods while the 16th Michigan pressed the Rebel front. Facing the 16th Michigan, Chambliss had dismounted his 10th Virginia Cavalry and part of the 9th in line of battle, while the rest of the 9th remained mounted in reserve. But the Confederate realized his precarious position and ordered his 13th Virginia Cavalry and one of Breathed's guns to withdraw. Chamberlain's flank attack drove a wedge between Chambliss' battle line and the retreating troopers. While the mounted troopers scattered, the dismounted Rebels were captured, and one of Breathed's guns was in jeopardy. Advancing with instructions to shoot the enemy's artillery horses to prevent removal, the men of the 118th Pennsylvania lost the prize when they found their advance blocked by a narrow but deep-looking stream. Impatient at the delay, Chamberlain urged them to take a nearby heavy plank fence with them and "throw it in, and yourselves after it!" But by this time, the Federals' movement had attracted the Rebel artillerymen's notice, and they whirled to greet the Union infantrymen with canister. The assault continued, dismounting four Confederate artillerymen and killing one, but much to the Federals' chagrin, Breathed's gun was limbered and escaped toward Bethany Church. Chamberlain and the men of the 118th Pennsylvania would have particular reason to regret their failure to take Breathed's gun. When the 5th Corps column continued its march, Breathed came in from behind, throwing shells into the 3rd Brigade column. Division commander Griffin personally deployed the parrotts, Battery D of the 5th U.S. Artillery. Though the rifled Federal guns easily dispersed the persistent Rebels, some of the 5th Corps' own men were killed by their fire.[8]

The 118th Pennsylvania and the 20th Maine had barely resumed their places in the 5th Corps' advancing line of battle when the commander of their skirmishers suddenly came upon a mounted Confederate major, seemingly oblivious to the troops advancing upon him. Chamberlain, also in advance of the line, silently turned and raised his hand to stop the line. Captain Walters of the 118th Pennsylvania circled around the self-absorbed officer in gray and called upon him to surrender. While the shocked Confederate officer agreed to surrender his pistol, when asked to surrender his sword, he drove it into the ground, breaking it off at the hilt. Chamberlain himself had almost become a victim of his own incaution when press-

LOC   MOLLUS, USAMHI

Gen. George Meade   Gen. Charles Griffin

ing another attack on May 21. He realized too late that he was within the enemy's lines. Throwing himself to the ground, Chamberlain made a narrow escape, drawing himself along by grassroots of an open field through sharp enemy fire.[9]

The Army of the Potomac was now moving through countryside that was refreshingly open and unspoiled after the tangle of the Wilderness, but while enjoying vistas unspoiled by the ravages of war, the Federals were still moving blindly. Rumor and the Rebel cavalry had delayed the 5th Corps' advance only one hour on May 22, but by the time Warren halted, as ordered at Harris' Store, the Army of Northern Virginia had reached Hanover Station in force. Grant was unsure of Lee's intentions, and the Army of the Potomac's orders for May 23 directed the corps commanders to send out what cavalry they had southward at dawn, with the corps to follow. As the four Federal corps approached the North Anna, it became apparent that the faulty maps they had been relying upon were worse than useless. Reconnaissance parties were not only feeling for the enemy, but they searched for roads that would bring the infantry forces that followed them to their assigned points on the North Anna. Mislabeled bridges, fords, and landmarks — miles off course on the Army of the Potomac maps —

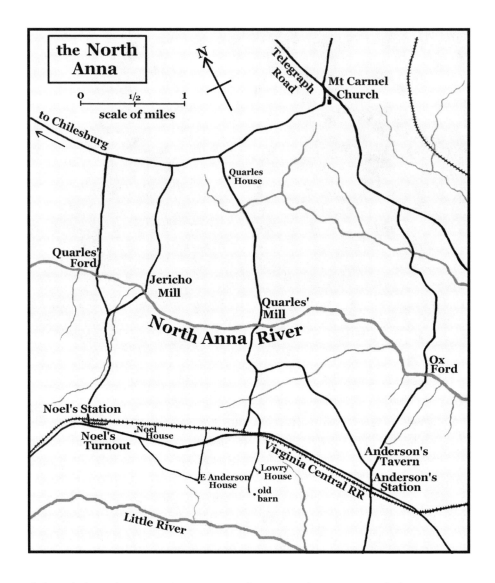

delayed the advance. Cooperation between the corps and their scouts, however, went a long way in untangling the mess. When it was discovered that the 5th Corps was occupying a road seemingly necessary for the 2nd Corps' approach to its assigned position, Warren gave way, though he was reduced to relying on the shaky recollection of an elderly slave who was acting as his guide. While Hancock encountered stiff opposition as he approached the North Anna, the 5th Corps moved down an old road that led, fortunately, to Jericho Mill. There was no bridge, only a dam with a ropes and rowboat ferry, but the spot was virtually undefended. Warren, realizing that his presence on the south side of the river would uncover all nearby crossings for the Federals, took the initiative to start crossing his men immediately. The banks were precipitous, some fifty to seventy-five feet high, and the water was armpit deep. But shortly after noon, the 2nd and 3rd Brigades waded across roughly 150 feet of the swiftly flowing North Anna. They dispersed a few home guards on the south bank and deployed to cover the construction of a pontoon bridge that would speed the 5th Corps' crossing and allow it to bring over artillery.[10]

The presence of an isolated Federal corps had not escaped the Rebels' notice. Confederate General Cadmus Marcellus Wilcox's Division, of General Ambrose Powell Hill's Corps, moved to meet the 5th Corps' incursion. While neither Grant nor Warren believed they would meet with much resistance on the North Anna, the position that the 5th Corps commander chose south of the river was a strong one. This was fortunate, for at 6 p.m., the Confederate attack hit the 5th Corps. It struck the right of Griffin's Division, established at the center of the line, and hit General Lysander Cutler's Division as it was moving into position on the right. Federal cavalry that had been sent out to guard the 5th Corps' right flank having come back in without orders, the Rebel assault on the 4th Division was a complete surprise. When most of Cutler's men broke and ran, a single battery under the command of Captain Charles E. Mink checked the Rebel pursuit. The outspoken commander of the 5th Corps artillery, Col. Charles Wainwright, brought up additional batteries and would claim that the artillery saved the 5th Corps that day. But they had some help from Griffin's 3rd Brigade, which had been lying in reserve behind the 1st Division line when the Rebel attack began. Colonel Jacob B. Sweitzer's 2nd Brigade, holding the right of the 1st Division line, was beginning to break when elements of the 3rd Brigade arrived just in time to add their weight and fire to Sweitzer's threatened flanks. While the 83rd Pennsylvania and 16th Michigan checked the flanking Rebels on Sweitzer's right, Chamberlain, commanding the 44th New York and the 118th Pennsylvania, filled the breach between the 2nd Brigade and the rest of the 1st Division. Advancing under heavy fire, when the men of the 118th Pennsylvania arrived at their position, they found the 44th New York lying down, so covered by leaves and underbrush as to be all but invisible. Chamberlain instructed the 118th to lie down immediately in the 44th's rear. With a view to making a countercharge, the instructions were that if the enemy attack should press in upon them, the 44th New York would rise up and fire a volley, then lie down. Then, the 118th Pennsylvania would deliver its fire, and with fixed bayonets charge over the 44th. Though the fighting spread along the rest of the 5th Corps line and continued until well after dark, it proved unnecessary for the 44th New York and 118th Pennsylvania to advance. Years later, George W. Carleton, an admiring veteran of the 20th Maine, described Chamberlain as he remembered him on the field that day. "The fire was tremendous but he persisted in standing out far in front of his men whom he ordered to lie down to keep out of fire while he watched the decisive moment to strike the foe — his officers — earnestly and affectionately urged him to take more shelter — but he replied `I am in no more danger than any other person would be here. It is necessary to know what is going on to meet the case promptly.'" Chamberlain would be embarrassed by this soldier's lavish praise, calling it a "panegyric." But while he commented that we might pardon Carleton's enthusiasm as one of the sort written by "...a soldier who is apt to think his commander `the' one," Chamberlain would contradict only a few of Carleton's facts and descriptions. The rapidness and volume of the fire of the 5th Corps' fight was heard four miles away at army headquarters, alerting them to the violence of the enemy attack. The 6th Corps, led by Union General Horatio Gouverneur Wright, was urged to move to their relief, but by the time Wright could offer any assistance, the 5th Corps had successfully repelled Wilcox and driven the Rebels back to the railroad.[11]

Though Lee was ill during his confrontation with Grant at the North Anna, the position he assumed was a masterly one. Forming his force into a V, holding only Ox Ford on the river, Lee, while still defending Hanover Junction, was so placed that Grant could not attack him without splitting his forces. As May 24 unfolded, the Federals would discover that the enemy's forces on both Hancock's front on the left and Warren's front on the right had fallen back, while all of Burnside's efforts to cross the river in the center were repulsed. When the 6th Corps crossed the North Anna to relieve Griffin's and Cutler's Divisions, Warren began an advance to the Virginia Central Railroad. At first the 5th Corps' movement was uncontested, but as the 20th Maine pressed beyond Noel's Station, it encountered Rebel sharpshooters taking cover in a stone barn. Chamberlain requested help from Captain Charles Phillips' 5th Massachusetts Battery, which arrived on the skirmish line with two guns. Ignoring the minié balls spattering around them, Phillips and his gun crews had soon set the barn afire, sending the Confederates back to their main line at Anderson's Tavern. During the night of May 24, orders were issued for the four corps of the Army of the Potomac, which now included the formerly independent command of Burnside's 9th Corps, to be prepared to advance and to again

LOC

Gen. Robert E. Lee

feel for the enemy's lines. It would become clear by the next day that Grant's assumption that Lee had withdrawn to the South Anna River was quite unfounded.[12]

Early on May 25, as Griffin's Division moved along the Virginia Central Railroad toward Anderson's Station, it encountered enemy skirmishers fighting stubbornly from behind logs and trees. One-half mile beyond these Rebel skirmishers was their main line, fronted by three-fourth mile of open field and covered by their artillery. As Griffin probed for weaknesses, one Federal skirmisher on the front that day described the fighting between the lines as "spiteful and continuous." But Warren's push against the Rebels on Lee's left flank was also protecting work parties sent to destroy as much of the Virginia Central Railroad as possible. In the afternoon, the 6th Corps came up on the right to assist in the destruction of the railroad, and while some five miles of track were destroyed, Roebling, Warren's sardonic aide and engineer, observed that the enemy could repair it in about ten days. By night, the entire 5th Corps line was entrenched. Under the cover of darkness, the 20th Maine advanced and silently threw up new works further to the front. Seemingly little had been accomplished that day, but the 5th Corps movement, in combination with a cavalry expedition to Little River further to the right, had been designed to give Lee reason to believe that the Army of the Potomac would move by its right flank in that direction. In that, the 5th Corps movement was apparently successful. Meanwhile, Grant, realizing that he was stalemated, would begin withdrawing his army from the North Anna the next day, but he would be moving his army by the left flank, driving toward Richmond.[13]

On May 26, Chamberlain had command of the picket line in front of the 1st Division where it confronted the Rebel entrenchments near Anderson's Tavern. During a day of torrential rains which drenched soldiers knee-deep in water in their trenches, orders were issued for the 5th Corps to begin its withdrawal from the lines after dark. Grant would describe it as "a delicate move to get the right wing of the Army of the Potomac from its position south of the North Anna in the presence of the enemy." While the 18th Massachusetts remained on the picket line, one by one, Chamberlain's regiments silently moved by the left to recross the river at Quarles' Mill. With the Rebels still apparently unaware of the Federal withdrawal, the 18th Massachusetts retired at about midnight to follow its brigade to the north bank. On reaching Mt. Carmel Church, the 5th Corps spent several hours issuing rations and allowing men of the 6th Corps to pass on their way, one of Wright's divisions accompanying Sheridan in a more than thirty mile movement toward the Pamunkey River near Hanovertown. That would be Warren's goal, too, but he would be moving by a longer route, unscouted and again inaccurately mapped. After stumbling through an intensely dark night with chilling rain that turned roads into ankle-deep mud, the men of the 5th Corps had an unpleasantly warm day for a march that would not end until sundown on May 27, when they

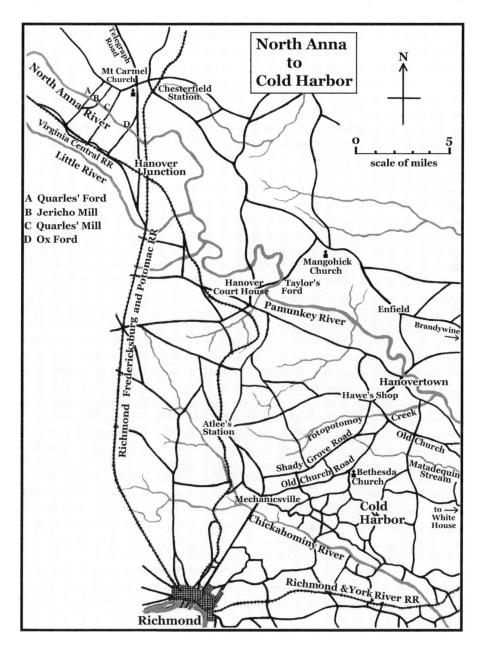

finally bivouacked near Mangohick Church, a short march from the
Pamunkey. The 2nd and 9th Corps had followed the 6th and 5th Corps
away from the North Anna, and at first light on May 27, the Rebels discovered that the Army of the Potomac had withdrawn. Lee was not unpre-
pared for such a movement, and by mid-morning the trenches at the North
Anna were silent and empty.[14]

There were many roads that passed over the Pamunkey and led to
Richmond. On the morning of May 28, Sheridan, with two divisions, was
sent out on the road that ran parallel to the Pamunkey to ascertain the
position of the enemy. But Confederate cavalry kept the Federal cavalry
more than a little busy throughout the day and well into the night. While
the Army of the Potomac had been put at a disadvantage for weeks by its
lack of cavalry, the only information Sheridan would provide this day was
that garnered from captured prisoners. Once again, the Army of the
Potomac was moving forward ignorant of Lee's whereabouts. The only
engagement for the 5th Corps on May 28 occurred when Meade and the
escort who preceded him approached their designated crossing near
Hanovertown on the Pamunkey. Here they discovered Rebel skirmishers
who had gotten between the Army of the Potomac's cavalry and infantry
forces. With the 3rd Brigade in the lead, Griffin's Division crossed over to
secure the area. After reconnoitering, Warren established an entrenched
line protecting the pontoon bridge for the 9th Corps following behind them,
while the 2nd and 6th Corps completed their passage on a crossing above.
Put simply, on May 28, while Sheridan battled Confederate cavalry to secure the roads that led from the Pamunkey to Richmond, Lee, behind his
screen of Rebel troopers, was maneuvering the Army of Northern Virginia
into position along a tributary of the Pamunkey, the Totopotomoy. When
the men of the Army of the Potomac moved blindly forward the next day,
they would find the Rebels waiting for them.[15]

On the morning of May 29, orders went out to the commanders of the
5th, 2nd, and 6th Corps, occupying the Army of the Potomac front from left
to right, respectively, to send out reconnaissance to be followed by their
whole corps. Meanwhile, the 9th Corps remained in reserve, and Sheridan's
Cavalry was watching the roads on the Army of the Potomac's left. Explor-
ing down diverging roads, the day's movement was one that would draw
the Federal infantry corps away from one another. Though the 6th Corps
encountered no resistance on the Federal right, Hancock, in the center,
would find the enemy well-entrenched on his front, barring the 2nd Corps
passage over the Totopotomoy. On the left, leading the 5th Corps, Griffin's

Division pushed the Rebel picket line before them, and with frequent and heavy skirmishing, crossed the stream. With Griffin alone across the Totopotomoy, the 5th Corps bivouacked for the night, and scouting offered ample proof that the enemy was ahead of them in force. Having observed some movement of the enemy toward their left, Warren's aide, Roebling, searched that night for the Federal troopers that were to have protected Warren's flank. Roebling failed to find a cavalry vedette closer than four miles away. On the morning of May 30, the Army of the Potomac Infantry Corps were again directed to close in upon the enemy in their respective fronts. On the far right, the 6th Corps would find such a tangle of swamp and woods, that it was unable to come up on Hancock's right until late in the day. The 2nd Corps, still confronting a strongly entrenched enemy, could only demonstrate. The 9th Corps was expected to come up between the 2nd and 5th Corps, and Warren had to rely on Burnside, not only to advance with him, but to relieve Warren's troops on the 5th Corps' right that were needed to protect the 5th's exposed left flank. Meanwhile, Warren refused to put much trust in the presence of cavalry, which, he had been assured, was watching things on the left, and he ordered his commanders to look out for themselves. Ultimately, when the 5th Corps advanced that morning, it did so virtually alone. Two 5th Corps divisions crossed the Totopotomoy to follow Griffin's Division. They moved several miles down Shady Grove Road, with Sweitzer's 2nd Brigade in the lead, feeling for the enemy. Upon entering a thickly wooded, marshy area called Magnolia Swamp, Confederate General Richard Stoddert Ewell's Corps was discovered behind sturdy earthworks on the opposite side of a swampy ravine.[16]

With the Rebels' main line discovered, Griffin extended his division into a line of battle to advance to meet the enemy. And the 3rd Brigade, under Chamberlain's command, was brought up under heavy fire to extend Sweitzer's line. Having to fight its way forward when the division advanced, the 3rd Brigade struck the main Rebel works, and was caught part way across an open field in a raking fire. Stubbornly, the men held their ground, trying to gain shelter by throwing up earth with their hands, bayonets, and tin plates. By mid-afternoon on May 30, it was becoming clear to Warren that he was still on his own across the Totopotomoy. While Hancock continued to face a strongly posted enemy in his front, Burnside's advance had failed to keep pace with the 5th Corps. Though the 5th Corps needed to make room for the 9th Corps at the front, and all corps were ordered to advance until striking the enemy, Burnside complained that

LOC

Gen. Ambrose Burnside

every time he made a connection with the men of the 5th Corps, they moved to the left or ahead. Burnside also protested against relieving any part of the 5th Corps, claiming that it would make his line too long. Meade apparently accepted Burnside's excuses, for he chided Warren for failing to notify Burnside of all 5th Corps movement. And, while some portion of Torbert's Cavalry Division was reported to be protecting the 5th Corps' left flank, Warren warned General Samuel Crawford, commanding on the 5th Corps left, not to count on cavalry cooperation. As the harassment he had experienced throughout the day from enemy cavalry on his left continued, Warren ordered Crawford's Brigade toward Bethesda Church in an effort to guard and support the left of his line. They arrived in time to receive a smashing flank attack by Maj. Gen. Robert Emmett Rodes' Division of Ewell's Corps. This drove Crawford's Pennsylvanians back to Shady Grove Road, where the Rebels were checked by Federal artillery.

Men of General Henry Hayes Lockwood's and Cutler's Divisions hurried to Crawford's assistance, and Warren repulsed General Jubal Anderson Early's determined attack, eventually driving the enemy back more than a mile. Warren informed army headquarters that he could hold his left, but he continued to ask, as he had all day, for the 9th Corps to move up and relieve his troops on the 5th Corps' right flank. But Burnside could not be found, and by the time reinforcements were sent, the fight was long over. It had been hoped that an assault Hancock had been ordered to make on his front would provide some relief for Warren, but the isolated 5th Corps had again had to survive a furious Rebel attack on its own. At dusk, Chamberlain, as general officer of outposts, started out to inspect his long picket line. Mistaking landmarks in this landscape of numerous swampy streams, he found himself within speaking distance of an enemy picket reserve. Observing the flurry of excitement his appearance had caused among the twenty or so Rebels, Chamberlain relied on a faded overcoat, darkness, and an assumed Southern accent to confuse the suspicious Confederates. Hoping to pass as one of their own officers who was making the rounds, Chamberlain called out to the gathering Rebels, "Never mind the guard. It's after sunset." Though he expected a bullet in his back at any moment, Chamberlain then proceeded to walk authoritatively across the Rebels' front, swerving to safety only when he had several sturdy oaks between him and the enemy rifles.[17]

On the morning of May 31, two divisions of Burnside's troops finally came up to relieve Warren's right, and all of Griffin's Division moved south of the Shady Grove Road. Chamberlain's men joined the right of Cutler's pickets, and a reconnaissance moved forward one-half mile to discover that the Rebels had withdrawn beyond Bethesda Church. Griffin's whole division moved up to his skirmishers' position to entrench near the new Rebel line. With orders for the entire Army of the Potomac to press forward against the enemy without an assault, (dubbed by one 3rd Brigade wag as one of "Grant's famous hugs"), it was not only determined that the enemy was too strongly positioned for an attack to be considered, but by this time, Grant's attention was already directed elsewhere. With General Benjamin Franklin Butler's entire force bottled up at Bermuda Hundred, Grant had called on the Army of the James for reinforcements. By May 31, General William F. [Baldy] Smith, having arrived by river transport with his 18th Corps, was marching from White House to join the Army of the Potomac. Sheridan's Cavalry took, relinquished, and retook the vital crossroads at Cold Harbor, as the Army of the Potomac began to sidle to the left with Wright's 6th Corps marching through the night from the army's far right to its left. Little would go right for Grant's plan for June 1. His staff misdirected Smith's movement, delaying his arrival for hours, and the 6th Corps was unable to reach Cold Harbor in time for the contemplated dawn attack.[18]

Lee, having anticipated that the Federals would move to their left, was observed at dawn on June 1 extending his own line to his right, each element of his battle line moving along its own front in that direction. Early in the morning, Warren extended his line toward the anticipated positions of the 6th and 18th Corps on his left, before he advanced and felt for the enemy in his front. Strung out in a single line some four miles long with little or no reserves, the 5th Corps began its advance. After circling around one of the many swamps created by the Totopotomoy and Matadequin streams in that area, the 3rd Brigade, under Chamberlain's command, took up a line half way up a ridge and began felling trees for breastworks. But the enemy soon discovered their work, and took steps to frustrate it. The 29th Massachusetts, thrown out as skirmishers, soon called on the 83rd Pennsylvania for reinforcements, for Rebels were discovered moving down a bushy ravine in preparation for a charge that would drive the Federals into the swamp behind them. But when the Rebels appeared at the top of the ridge, Chamberlain's men delivered a volley from their hastily constructed breastworks that sent the attackers reeling. Yet the stubborn Confederates had taken possession of some of the 29th Massachusetts' rifle pits, and had to be driven back to their own line. At mid-morning, it was observed that the Confederate movement to the right was continuing, and though Warren's troops faced the same enemy entrenchments that had been deemed impregnable on May 31, he was ordered to attack. Cutler's and Lockwood's Divisions, delayed by an imposing wooded swamp, then crossed open ground under heavy artillery fire, able to do no more then drive in the enemy's pickets. At 6 p.m. on June 1, under galling fire, the long awaited main attack at Cold Harbor began. The 6th Corps, while gaining part of the enemy's main line, could not hold it, and the 18th Corps could only take Rebel rifle pits. Both Federal corps retired with heavy losses.[19]

During the afternoon of June 1, Hancock was ordered to move from the extreme right of the army to its left to take part in a dawn attack at Cold Harbor. But Grant's plans were again plagued with problems. A long march was made longer by an errant staff guide, and the 2nd Corps arrived exhausted at Cold Harbor well after dawn on June 2. When it was learned that the 18th Corps, which had been ordered to march without its trains, was almost out of ammunition, the attack was postponed until 5 p.m. The 5th Corps, now holding a line nearly five miles long, soon received orders to which both Warren and Burnside objected. Burnside was ordered to withdraw his corps from the extreme Federal right to mass behind Warren, to act as his reserve, and protect the army's flank. Warren was directed to simultaneously extend his left flank to connect with Smith while contracting his right to make one-half of his force available as a reserve for the 5 p.m. attack. This was an assault Warren would be expected to make with the other corps. But Lee was not idle as the Army of the Potomac developed its plan of assault. Early, who was commanding Ewell's Corps, was ordered to get on the Army of the Potomac right and drive the Federals across the Army of Northern Virginia front. While early in the afternoon of June 2, the Army of the Potomac's 5 p.m. attack was postponed until the following morning, orders for the 5th and 9th Corps movement were retained. Burnside's withdrawal began at 3 p.m. in the midst of a severe thunderstorm, with the enemy following him closely and driving in 9th Corps pickets before their intended recall. On the 5th Corps right, before 3rd Brigade pickets were even aware that the 9th Corps withdrawal had begun, the Rebels appeared between the skirmish line and their main line, gobbling up a sizable number of the amazed Federals. Griffin's Division, massed near Bethesda Church in preparation for its movement to the left, dropped back to a better position to meet the advancing Rebels. Chamberlain, having returned to command the 20th Maine, was compelled to fight his way through the encircling Rebels. Coming in at the double-quick, Chamberlain earned Bartlett's admiration when asked at this crisis in the battle to take his men back into the maelstrom. Bartlett effusively praised Chamberlain's swift and efficient orders which, though given under fire, brought the regiment back into the fight. Once the enemy attack had been repulsed, Griffin deployed in a line of battle with Bartlett's Brigade in the center, advancing under heavy musket and artillery fire to attack Rode's Division, forcing it back to Shady Grove Road. The 3rd Brigade dug in under fire for a fight that would continue until dark. That proud private of the 20th Maine once more recorded his memory of Chamberlain, who again stood beyond his entrenchments fully exposed to a heavy artillery fire while watching the enemy. Carleton tells that this time the men could stand it no longer, and several of the regiment's sergeants actually took their commander by main force, compelling Chamberlain to join his men in the trenches. Grant, in his memoirs, not only makes no mention of the

LOC

Gen. Joseph J. Bartlett

miles of front Warren was covering with a single line, but also fails to acknowledge Griffin's countercharge that day. Grant remarked, "While Warren and Burnside were making these charges the enemy came out several times and attacked them capturing several hundred prisoners. The attacks were repulsed but not followed up as they should have been. I was so annoyed at this that I directed Meade to instruct his corps commanders that they should seize all such opportunities when they occurred, and not wait for orders, all of our maneuvers being made for the very purpose of getting the enemy out of his cover."[20]

Because the Rebels cut off communications between the 5th Corps and army headquarters, results of the fight on the Army of the Potomac right were not known until, in the gathering darkness, Warren sent Roebling to report to Meade. Both Warren's and Roebling's reports for June 2 express their frustration regarding the difficulties of coordinating intricate or potentially confusing orders for movement with Burnside. But Roebling conveyed a good deal more than recriminations over the pounding the 5th

Corps had endured that day. Having scouted clear out to the exposed and vulnerable Rebel left flank in front of the 9th Corps, Roebling had knowledge of an important opportunity. Warren asked nothing less than for Meade himself to come to the army's right to direct an attack, or give Warren command of the 5th and 9th Corps to attack the vulnerable Rebels should they be there in the morning. Meade had other plans for the morning of June 3, but he was interested enough to send Roebling to Grant. Though Grant was not oblivious to opportunities on the right, he expressed the binding opinion that it would be inappropriate for Burnside to be subject to Warren's orders. Roebling carried back word to Warren that he and Burnside were to cooperate, and, as previously ordered, all corps would be expected to assault as ordered on their front at 4:30 a.m. the next day. Though the Army of the Potomac had and would experience many difficult days, June 3 was indeed a tragic one for that army. The 2nd, 6th, and 18th Corps threw themselves against breastworks which the Rebels had had many hours to prepare. On the Union right, Griffin's Division, with the challenging assignment of maintaining the connection between the 5th and 9th Corps, swung back to connect with Burnside's line. The 5th Corps waited two hours for the 9th to "cooperate," with the assault finally made around 6:30 a.m. The 20th Maine advanced under heavy fire with the 3rd Brigade at the center of the 1st Division's line of battle. While statistics may lose their significance in this day of staggering Federal losses, Chamberlain's regiment suffered twenty-four of the estimated 400 casualties that the 5th Corps incurred. While the left and center of the strung out 5th Corps line confronted men of Anderson's Corps, the rest of the 5th Corps and elements of the 9th Corps faced Ewell's Corps and part of Hill's Corps, still in force on Shady Grove Road. Though the Rebels awaited the Federal advance behind newly constructed breastworks, they were forced back. Burnside, who had regained much of his old position, had another attempt to get around the enemy's left flank scheduled for 2 p.m., but it was called off by army headquarters for unknown reasons. A bitter Roebling suggested, "perhaps because there was a prospect of success." During the night, the men of Ewell's and Hill's Corps were pulled back.[21]

With the discovery that the enemy had disappeared from Burnside's front and drawn back from Warren's, on June 4 the 9th Corps was moved to the left to take up a position between the 5th and 18th Corps. The 5th Corps, now holding the extreme right of the army, received orders that it would be withdrawn to the rear after dark on June 5, to take up a position in reserve near Cold Harbor. Before the movement, Warren had the temerity to address General James Wilson, commander of the cavalry division on his right, noting that none of Wilson's troopers were closer than two miles from the infantry. While asking if Wilson had orders to give him notice of enemy movement on his right, Warren referred to the cavalry's failure to alert the 5th Corps of the enemy's attack on Warren's left on May 30. Sheridan's and Wilson's surly replies, transmitted through Army of the Potomac headquarters, did not bode well for the cooperation Warren could expect from the cavalry in the coming days. Griffin's Division was the last to withdraw shortly before dawn on June 6. Major Ellis Spear was left in command of the 20th Maine and the 1st Division pickets.

Though several of the 1st Division's regimental officers were senior to him, on June 5 Chamberlain was given command of the newly formed 1st Brigade. Chamberlain inherited five regiments of old 1st Corps veterans which had been serving in Cutler's Division: the 121st, 142nd, 143rd, 149th and the 150th Pennsylvania. On June 6, a newly arrived regiment was added. The 187th Pennsylvania had more than 800 men, outnumbering the survivors of the other five regiments combined. Warren, on giving Chamberlain brigade command, also urged his promotion to brigadier general of volunteers.[22]

After a successful withdrawal, the 5th Corps welcomed this opportunity to be away from the unremitting stress of the front lines, and for the first time since it had left the Rapidan, the corps' baggage train was brought up with its promise of clean clothing and supplies. Both officers and men were filthy, and it was impossible to keep free of lice. But Burnside's repeated nervous calls for assistance for his 9th Corps, now holding the army's right, led to orders that sent the 5th Corps train away. It was a short rest for the 1st Division, for late on the night of June 6, orders were issued for Griffin's and Cutler's Divisions to march at 3:30 a.m. on June 7 to the Chickahominy to guard river crossings on the 2nd Corps' left. Bivouacked about a mile from the river, here some of the 1st Brigade would find moments of relaxation, even while pulling duty on the picket line. The men of the 150th Pennsylvania found themselves opposite the 24th Georgia, Rebels they had had a pacific relationship with earlier in the spring below Fredericksburg. But when the Bucktails discovered a bee tree, the sound of their axes brought a threat from Rebel officers that they would fire. Bringing the tree down a few strokes at a time, the entire Federal picket line enjoyed the spoils. Further entertainment was provided when the Rebels brought up a railroad monitor, a rifled thirty-two pounder. A former ordinance officer speculated that the 300-pound shells the Rebels were throwing at them were those taken from the Federals at Plymouth, North Carolina. The new boys of the 187th Pennsylvania found the fire from the enemy's batteries nothing less than terrifying, but they would also be treated to one of the more romantic amenities of military life when they participated in a dress parade several days later. And Chamberlain would also take advantage of moments of inactivity to put his inexperienced new regiment through the all too necessary drudgery of drill.[23]

On June 8, Grant, Meade, and Warren spent some time studying a map, spread out on the grass beneath an apple tree. There was a great deal to talk about, for Grant was planning the withdrawal of the Army of the Potomac from Cold Harbor to execute a daring passage across the Chickahominy and the James Rivers for the investment of Petersburg and Richmond. This very day, an expedition from the Army of the James advanced on Petersburg, while one of Grant's aides was on his way to choose the site where the Army of the Potomac would cross the James to join Butler's forces. Confidentially informed of the screening role the 5th Corps would play in the Army of the Potomac's march to the James, Warren knew the importance of preventing the enemy from observing the movement of his remaining two divisions still lying near Cold Harbor toward the Chickahominy on the night of June 11. The 5th Corps was uniting to cross the river at Long Bridge after dark on June 12, with orders to move out to Quaker Road or until stopped by the enemy. The 2nd Corps would follow the 5th Corps, while the 6th and 9th Corps crossed lower down at Jones Bridge. With the 5th Corps screening the army's movement, the 2nd, 6th and 9th Corps would march to Fort Powhatan on the James, while Smith's 18th Corps would return to the Army of the James by water.[24]

All did not go as planned on the night of June 12. The 5th Corps was to be preceded by Wilson's Cavalry, which was expected to effect a crossing at Long Bridge and construct a pontoon bridge. The leading division of the 5th Corps upon reaching Long Bridge at 10 p.m. found the cavalry just arriving, and the infantry settled down to wait. Wilson's skirmishers fought for an hour before securing the crossing so that work on a pontoon bridge could begin, delaying passage over the Chickahominy until 1 a.m. on June 13. Things did not go smoothly for all of Chamberlain's new 1st Brigade. A picket line, left on the Chickahominy while the 1st Division marched along the river road to Long Bridge, should have been notified by the officer in charge around midnight to withdraw. By 2 a.m. or 3 a.m. on the morning of June 13, members of both the 150th and 187th Pennsylvania realized that they had been left behind and were in danger of capture.

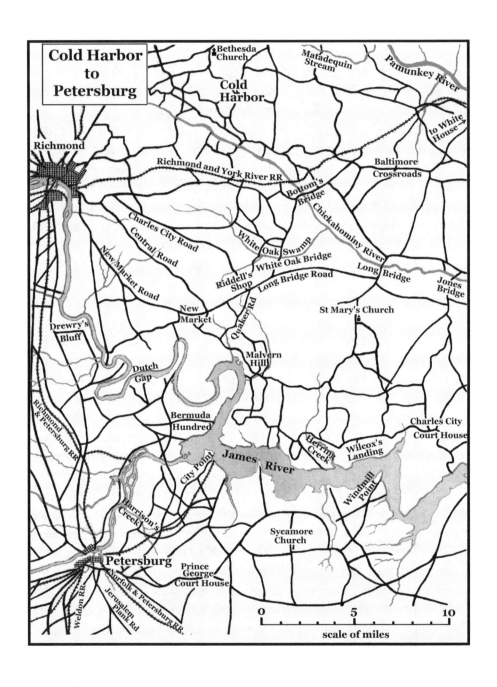

Posted in a swamp, they became lost in the darkness, floundering through knee-deep mire until knowledge of a line of pursuing Rebels lent wings to their feet. Skirmishing with the enemy and taking their best guess at the direction their division had gone, it was near midnight before many of the disgruntled soldiers could confront the officer who had left them to their fate. One unit history notes that the unnamed officer was later tried and dismissed from the service for cowardice.[25]

Once across the river, obstructions on Long Bridge Road caused further delays, and it was nearly daylight by the time Crawford's Division followed Wilson's Cavalry. After two miles, Crawford formed a line of battle, while the rest of the 5th Corps massed behind him, guarding various roads and fords. Once again coping with inaccurate maps, Warren found it necessary to send Roebling in search for a direct road by which the 5th Corps would later follow the Army of the Potomac to the James. Meanwhile, Wilson's Cavalry, skirmishing with Rebel horsemen, pushed on to a crossroads at New Market followed by Crawford's force which dug in at White Oak Swamp Bridge. Once Lee had discovered that the Army of the Potomac was gone from its entrenchment at Cold Harbor, he crossed the Chickahominy, moving toward Richmond. Anderson's and Hill's Corps came up late in the day to confront the 5th Corps and ply the Federals with artillery. But the effectiveness of the 5th Corps' position was its salvation. While Lee realized they might merely be screening a Federal move to the James, the Rebel commander could not be sure that Warren was not the Army of the Potomac advance moving toward Richmond on Long Bridge Road. In the gathering darkness, Lee concluded that he would attack the next day, but Warren safely withdrew during the night, followed by Wilson's Cavalry. Friction developed between the exhausted infantrymen and troopers as they followed the Army of the Potomac, when one of Wilson's brigade commanders, General John B. McIntosh, pushed ahead of the infantry with his horsemen, blocking the road. The 5th Corps marched far into the night but made it only as far as St. Mary's Church, for the troopers, in addition to blocking the road, considered it a good joke to throw cartridges into their fires to alarm passing infantrymen, causing them to prepare for an attack.[26]

Chamberlain's regiments were moving well into the early hours of June 14, and as day broke and the cavalry was finally gotten out of the way, the 1st Brigade marched with the 5th Corps to Charles City Court House. Arriving at noon, they bivouacked near Court House Creek. The men of the 3rd Brigade occupied the trenches that the 2nd Corps had thrown up, while the 6th and 9th Corps began to arrive and mass around the picturesque little town. So far, Grant's daring movement had gone exceptionally well, but serious delays began to mar this masterly plan. The pontoon bridge, an engineering marvel necessary for the trains and cavalry to cross the James, would not be completed until near midnight. The bridge by which the army trains were to cross the Chickahominy and follow the army proved too short to span the river. Many who waited near the banks of the James throughout the day of June 14 were aware that such delays might cost them victory at the end of their remarkable march. As the 2nd Corps began crossing the river on steamboats, Grant traveled to Bermuda Hundred to initiate an offensive by elements of Butler's Army of the James against Petersburg. Returning by water from its fight at Cold Harbor, Smith's 18th Corps would make the assault. He was supported by General Edward W. Hinks' Division of U.S. Colored Troops and General August V. Kautz's Cavalry Division, a combined force of 18,000 men. It seems evident from the official records that Grant had every confidence that Smith, his former chief engineer from the West, would make short work of Petersburg, a transportation hub vital to Richmond's survival. While orders were issued for the Army of the Potomac to proceed to within supporting distance of Smith's effort, no urgency was expressed. After the fact, when Smith's attack late in the day on June 15 fell far short of securing the city, insinuations began that Meade and Hancock had misunderstood their role in the assault.

Without question, things went very wrong. Though the fortifications at Petersburg were strong and imposing, at the time of Smith's attack its seven-and-one-half-mile line was defended by only 2,200 men. In his memoirs many years later, Grant still seemed baffled over the failure, stating, "I believed then, and still believe, that Petersburg could have been easily captured at that time." Though Hancock's Corps had crossed the James by dawn on June 15, he had orders from Meade to wait at Windmill Point for the rations Grant had ordered Butler to send from Bermuda Hundred. But that was not the only problem. The 2nd Corps was ordered to advance to a position on Harrison's Creek where it intersected with the City Point Railroad. While Army of the Potomac maps showed that location to be three-and-one-half miles east of Petersburg, it was actually located within the city and its Rebel-held fortifications. Hancock did not receive word until 5:30 p.m. that he was expected to support Smith's assault, and by the time he was able to bring up part of his force, Smith was not inclined to continue the attack.[27]

LOC

Gen. William Farrar (Baldy) Smith

LOC

Gen. Winfield Scott Hancock, seated,
with Gens. Francis Barlow, David Birney, and John Gibbon

As soon as the Federal withdrawal from Cold Harbor had been discovered on June 13, Lee had suspected that Grant was headed south of the James. But the screen that the 5th Corps, and in succeeding days the Federal cavalry, had maintained between the Army of Northern Virginia and the Army of the Potomac, kept Lee in doubt of his enemy's objectives. Though the 5th Corps had vanished from his front during the night of June 14, uncertainty kept the Rebel army for several days in its position at the White Oak Swamp. Lee also realized Petersburg's vulnerability, and that district's commander, General Pierre Gustave Toutant Beauregard, was calling for the return of his troops that had been detached to reinforce the Army of Northern Virginia. On June 15, Lee therefore sent General Robert F. Hoke's Brigade and shifted one of Anderson's Brigades to allow General Robert Ransom to return to Beauregard. With Smith's attack on Petersburg, Hoke's and Ransom's Brigades would provide much needed relief for the beleaguered defenders. But the continuing mystery of the Army of the Potomac's whereabouts stalled any decisive effort on Lee's part to go to Petersburg's defense. In desperation, on June 16, Beauregard stripped his force confronting Butler at Bermuda Hundred, some 4,500 men, in order to man the Petersburg defenses. On that day, Lee raced Pickett's Division forward to regain the Rebel entrenchments facing the Army of the James, while Anderson's Division moved to Malvern Hill in support. As Lee's attention was occupied with putting Butler back in his bottle, fewer than 11,000 men manned the defenses of Petersburg. It would seem that Grant still had the time and the means to take the city, but it did not happen. Late on the night of June 15, Grant sent Meade orders to rush another corps to Petersburg and advised Hancock and Smith to take up a defensive position until more of the Army of the Potomac arrived at Petersburg. On the morning of June 16, with a remarkable abdication of responsibility, Grant left the ailing Hancock in command of the force in front of Petersburg and sent orders for Meade to come up at once to take command of the assault which Grant had ordered for 6 p.m.[28]

While the 9th Corps marched through the night of June 15-16 toward Petersburg, the 5th Corps was under orders to cross the James at daybreak on June 16. Well before dawn, the men moved down to the river. At Wilcox's Landing, Chamberlain saw his 1st Brigade begin boarding the transport *Exchange* and the tugboat *Eliza Hancock*. Disembarking at Windmill Point, they received two days' rations from the ironclad *Atlanta*. As the rest of the 5th Corps crossed, the men of the 1st Division, armed with soap, waded into the river, clothes and all, to wash off six weeks of grime. Receiv-

LOC

Gen. Pierre Gustave Toutant Beauregard

ing orders to proceed to Petersburg with all possible speed, by 1 p.m. the 5th Corps was on the march under a scorching sun, the dust from the powder-dry road rising in choking clouds. Those who had passed up filling their canteens from pools covered with green slime would regret it, for that was the only water that would be found along the route. During the march, the only Federal cavalry at Petersburg, under the command of Kautz, sent a warning to Warren that he might well meet Rebels before he reached the city. The 5th Corps veered from the route Burnside had taken, moving instead through Sycamore Church and Prince George Court House. At sundown, Chamberlain's 1st Brigade was allowed to stop to eat and make coffee near Prince George Court House. They hoped that their exhausting day was over, but the bugles rang out for the march to continue. At midnight, June 16-17, they reached a position some distance behind the men of the 9th Corps. Those men of the 1st Brigade who were not pressed ahead to act as skirmishers dropped in their tracks. They were oblivious in their sleep to the rifle fire that reached their bivouac throughout the night from the front. After a brief consultation with Kautz, the horsemen who had guarded the Army of the Potomac's left flank departed to return to Butler. Warren spent the rest of the night examining the ground and the lines at Petersburg and conferring with his fellow corps commanders.[29]

Well before the weary men of the 5th Corps neared Petersburg, they could hear the fight going on during the evening and night of June 16. The long-awaited 9th Corps had begun arriving at Petersburg at midday, the exhausted men filing into position near the 2nd Corps during the afternoon. But the 2nd Corps would bear the primary burdens of the assault. While Grant returned to City Point, his engineers, Generals John G. Barnard and Cyrus B. Comstock, whom Grant left at Petersburg to advise Hancock and Meade, asserted that they were unable to establish the strength of the enemy anywhere on the line except on Hancock's front. They suggested that the 2nd Corps attack on its front, while elements of the 9th Corps were held in support, ready to advance in case of success. On Hancock's right, Smith, who had withdrawn from the position he had taken on June 15, had

LOC

Gen. August Kautz

by that time reversed his opinion that those works could be easily retaken, and the 18th Corps was ordered to demonstrate and provide reserves. With dust hanging heavily in the air, Meade's forces moved into position. The descending sun turned an ominous copper-red, the color intensifying with smoke from the cannonade that preceded the Federal attack. With heavy losses, Hancock's assault drove the enemy some distance and held, though Rebel attacks continued through the night in futile attempts to retake the lost position. Encouraged by this success, and clinging to reports that Lee had yet to bring the Army of Northern Virginia to Beauregard's relief, Meade ordered Burnside to prepare for an assault across the moonlit landscape from his position on the 2nd Corps' left. Having reported Army of the Potomac actions for June 16, late that night Meade requested directions for the next day. Grant, from his headquarters at City Point, pleaded ignorance of the conditions on Meade's front and declined to give any positive directions regarding the assault on Petersburg. In the hours before dawn on June 17, elements of the 9th Corps advanced, supported by the 2nd Corps, to surprise the weary Petersburg defenders and take another portion of the Rebel fortifications.[30]

Daylight of June 17 brought Meade's order to the 5th Corps to be prepared to act in reserve for prospective 2nd and 9th Corps advances, while maintaining a position on Burnside's left to protect the Army of the Potomac's flank. Meade waited impatiently for detailed reports of the morning's gains to make preparations for a renewal of his assault, while Grant's attention was centered upon the Army of the James. Butler was falling back before Lee's forces from the position he had assumed after the Rebel withdrawal from his front on June 16. Should this ground be lost, any hope of driving a permanent wedge between Beauregard and Lee's forces and between Richmond and Petersburg would be lost with it. But instead of examining conditions at the front himself, Grant remained at City Point and sent another of his engineers, Lt. Col. Orville Babcock, to consider the situation. Having already promised that several divisions of Wright's 6th Corps would be diverted from coming to the Petersburg front to reinforce Butler, Grant also began repeating his request to Meade that Smith's 18th Corps be relieved from its position at Meade's front and returned to the Army of the James. At midday, Babcock informed Grant that he and Butler's engineer, General Godfrey Weitzel, concurred that the ground lost could and should be retaken. But before this could be effected, a smashing Confederate attack regained the Rebels' former line. Late in the afternoon, Butler requested direction from Grant, but Grant had finally left to pay a visit to Petersburg, and some little time passed before he directed Butler to attack. Butler ordered General Alfred Howe Terry to attack, along with Wright's 6th Corps in support. Terry was in temporary command of the Army of the James' 10th Corps. But both Terry and Wright recommended to Butler that, while they might be able to re-take the line, they would not be able to hold it. Butler's reiterated orders to attack were ignored, and any advantage that had been within the Army of the James' grasp was lost.[31]

During the afternoon of June 17 at Petersburg, another of Burnside's Divisions, in conjunction with elements of the 2nd Corps, advanced with some success against the new line of earthworks the enemy had thrown up during the night. Subsequent reconnaissance on the Army of the Potomac left near the Norfolk Pike [also known as the Sussex or Baxter

LOC

Gen. Benjamin Butler

Road] revealed that the Rebel line, which ran in front of a large pin-ewood, seemed to be lightly held. It was impossible to know what force lay in the woods. Around noon, Crawford's and Griffin's Divisions, as Burnside's reserves, advanced to the 9th Corps' rear, forming their line just behind the enemy entrenchments that the 9th Corps had taken the night before. Cutler's Division was placed in line to the rear and left of the 9th Corps, a position confronting the Rebel-held Avery House, while Cutler's left extended to the Norfolk Railroad. Roebling spent the afternoon pushing a reconnaissance farther to the left, circling around to and moving up the Jerusalem Plank Road toward the enemy fortifications until encountering Confederate General James Dearing's Cavalry, which effectively screened the Rebel right. Just before dark, another of Burnside's Divisions, by heavy fighting, succeeded in getting across the Rebel line. After dark, Crawford's Division near the Avery House received orders to advance. Though starting well, the lines of Crawford's 3rd Division disintegrated while trying to move through two ravines. When these lines were restored, Crawford's men had apparently lost all sense of direction. Yet when the right of his line struck the Rebel entrenchments, sixty surprised Confederates and a battle flag were captured before Crawford's Division became hopelessly intermixed with the 9th Corps attackers. Eventually, the entire Federal advance fell back through the darkness. The fighting on June 17 was over with none of the day's costly Federal gains by the 2nd, 5th, and 9th Corps having been held. Well before news of the withdrawal became known at army headquarters, Meade urged Warren, should there be any successes, to form his whole corps for a night attack. But within a half hour of this directive, Meade was urging caution, suggesting to his 5th Corps commander that unless a most promising situation existed, he should hold onto what he had and let his men rest for a proposed dawn attack the next day. It was well into June 18 before Warren or Meade would know that none of the dearly-bought Federal advances of the 17th had been held.[32]

Not until the night of June 17 did Lee begin to commit the Army of Northern Virginia to the defense of Petersburg. In the days leading up to June 17, Lee's dispatches make it clear that neither he nor Beauregard knew where all the corps of the Army of the Potomac were, and that Lee would not leave his Drewry's Bluff position and the defense of Richmond without definite information. But, on the night of June 17, when Lee received information convincing him that the Army

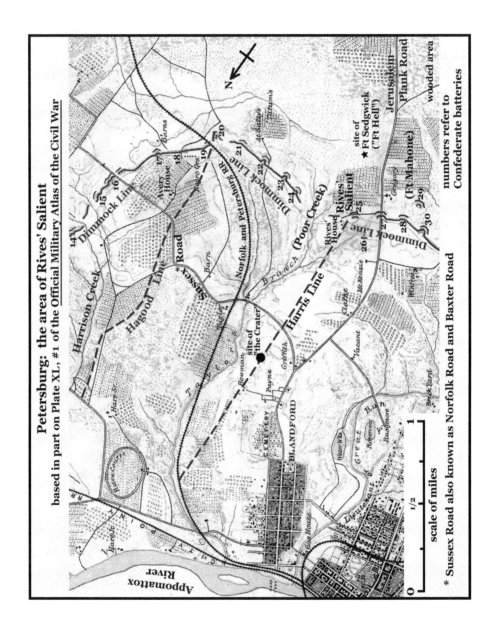

Petersburg: the area of Rives' Salient
based in part on Plate XL, #1 of the Official Military Atlas of the Civil War

of the Potomac was across the James and at Petersburg, he took steps to bring his army to the city's relief. Before dawn on June 18, two divisions of Anderson's [Longstreet's] Corps, some 10,000 soldiers, began their movement to Petersburg, with the rest of the army to follow. One soldier of General Charles W. Field's Division perhaps described it best as first starting as a forced march, but before daylight turning into a run, for "from the manner we were urged forward it was evident that our troops somewhere were in imminent peril." And indeed, the exhausted defenders of Petersburg were in desperate straights. Leaving a strong picket line and bright fires burning on the center and left of their line, the Rebels pulled back closer to the city and began to entrench their third and final line. On Beauregard's right, much of the formidable fortifications of the original Dimmock Line stood empty. But at 7:30 a.m. on June 18, Lee's advance, General Joseph B. Kershaw's Division, arrived at Petersburg. His division was placed in the trenches southeast of Blandford Cemetery, the division's right resting in the original Dimmock Line fortifications at Rives' Salient and on the Jerusalem Plank Road. Two hours later, Field's Division arrived and by midday was placed on Kershaw's right. The defenses on the Confederate right, which since June 15 had remained vulnerable and unguarded from west and north of the Jerusalem Plank Road to the Appomattox, were being manned, but Meade had no knowledge of the arrival of these advance forces of the Army of Northern Virginia. Believing that the defenders of Petersburg had neither been reinforced nor had had the time to strengthen their new line, Meade urged haste. In what has been described as a tearing humor, and seemingly oblivious to the distances and obstacles the left of his attack force faced, Meade pressed his corps commanders to report when ready for a simultaneous assault.[33]

Here, let us join an annotated version of Chamberlain's "Charge at Fort Hell" where we will follow the fate of the 1st Brigade, 1st Division, 5th Corps, and the Army of the Potomac through the fighting on June 18, 1864.

THE CHARGE AT FORT HELL
JUNE 18, 1864
BY JOSHUA LAWRENCE CHAMBERLAIN

We made a forced march over the James, and to the Petersburg front; but we wasted the whole day, so that we lost the end for which this severe march was inflicted on the men — cheerfully carried through by them out of their loyalty and heartiness.[1]

My brigade was a splendid one; given [or made up especially for] me in consideration of my losing my old, Third Brigade through my misfortune at Rappahannock Station, where after the heat of the assault I had taken a night's bivouac on the bare ground and under an open sky, in a damp, driving snow storm. Returning from Georgetown Seminary Hospital, I found my brigade in [the] command of General Bartlett of the Sixth Corps.[2]

This First Brigade, however, made up to me the loss. It was composed of five regiments from the old First Corps, remnants of Chapman Biddle's and Roy Stone's Brigades, of Doubleday's old Division, and the splendid new regiment, the 187th Pennsylvania; six regiments as good as ever took arms. Veterans, in fact, the five old regiments, having passed through untold hardships and slaughter at Gettysburg, and in truth, some of them looked upon as somewhat shorn of their honor there as well as of their numbers, by reason of not holding on after all was lost — or perhaps for holding on until one of them lost their colors. At any rate, I found them somewhat disheartened when I took them, after Cold Harbor, and I set to work to restore their spirit, and discipline, and assured them I would recover their prestige in the first battle we went into.[3]

On the night of the 17th they all lay out on the ground before the outer works of Petersburg — 2,500 or 3,000 men — waiting for the fierce attack

---

1. For a detailed description of the 5th Corps and the AoP's movement from Cold Harbor to Petersburg, see the introduction, pp. 33-41. Chamberlain's comment that they "wasted a whole day" at the Petersburg front likely refers to the fact that the 2nd and 18th Corps had been present at Petersburg since the night of June 15, yet no assault was made until 6 p.m. on June 16, and then by only one corps. But if Chamberlain's "we" refers to his brigade, division, or corps, he may have been pointing out that although the 5th Corps arrived near Petersburg around midnight on the night of June 16, it would not be fully engaged until midday on June 18.

2. On June 6, 1864, Chamberlain was assigned to command the newly formed 1st Brigade of the 1st Division, 5th Corps. Chamberlain had served intermittently as temporary commander of the 3rd Brigade, 1st Division, 5th Corps in the latter weeks of July 1863 until, after medical leave from the army from August 3 to August 24, he was assigned by Griffin to the command of the 3rd Brigade on August 26, 1863. At Rappahannock Station, a spirit of comradeship involved Chamberlain's 3rd Brigade in an attack on the Rebel earthworks that was, in fact, supposed to be a 6th Corps' show. When 20th Maine skirmishers got wind of an attack to be made by the 6th Maine on their flank, the urge to help these boys from Maine proved irresistible to about eighty members of the 20th. Chamberlain retained command of the 3rd Brigade until mid-November, when the symptoms of an illness he had been suffering with for several weeks became acute. Sent unconscious by cattle car to Washington, D.C., where he was admitted to Georgetown Seminary Hospital, his illness was diagnosed as typho-malarial fever. Chamberlain remained hospitalized until granted leave, arriving at his Brunswick home on December 18. In early February 1864, sufficiently recovered for light duty, he began serving on court-martial in Washington, D.C.; Baltimore; and Trenton, New Jersey, serving through the months of March, April, and the first weeks of May. Though having had a reappearance of malarial symptoms in mid-April, by the end of that month, Chamberlain requested to be returned to duty in the field. Upon learning that his letter never arrived at the Adjutant General's Office in Washington, he repeated his request for relief from court-martial duty on May 9 and it was granted the next day. The diary of a soldier of the 20th Maine, recuperating from a wound in a Washington, D.C., hospital, records that Chamberlain left the capitol on May 16, and Chamberlain's personal records state he returned to duty on May 18. However, Chamberlain also described a special command he was given within an hour of his return to the 5th Corps. On consideration of the official records and the accounts of the units that participated in the described action, it must be assumed that Chamberlain returned to the army in the last hours of May 17. Bartlett, a brigadier general with experience commanding a division in the 6th Corps, had been given permanent command of Chamberlain's 3rd Brigade on April 3, 1864. But due to Bartlett's illness, Chamberlain was placed in command of the brigade several times before he was assigned to command a newly formed 1st Brigade. Bartlett was subject to severe bouts of rheumatism that periodically disabled him, but there is also some evidence that he may have been suffering from the effects of a severe fall with his horse at the Wilderness. For details of Chamberlain's 5th Corps commands during the Overland Campaign before his assignment in June 1864 to the new 1st Brigade, 1st Division, see the introduction, pp. 8-32.

3. Five regiments from the old 1st Corps, the 121st, 142nd, 143rd, 149th, and 150th Pennsylvania had been assigned to the 4th Division, 5th Corps during the reorganization of the AoP in the spring of 1864. In June of 1864, they had been serving under Cutler, himself a former brigade & division commander in the 1st Corps, when they were transferred on June 6, 1864, to the new 1st Brigade in Griffin's 1st Division of 5th Corps. It was the 149th that lost its colors. The 121st and 142nd Pennsylvania had served in Col. Chapman Biddle's 1st Brigade, in General Thomas Rowley's 3rd Division, 1st Corps. Rowley took command of the division at Gettysburg when General Abner Doubleday ascended to command of the 1st Corps while General John Reynolds commanded the army's left wing. The 121st Pennsylvania lost 170 officers and men at Gettysburg; the 142nd lost 211 men. Though Rowley was cited in Doubleday's after-battle report for bravery, he was later found guilty by a court-martial of being under the influence of alcohol at Gettysburg.

LOC

Company D, 149th Pennsylvania Infantry

we were expecting to make in the morning on the enemy's defensive works, now well strengthened and manned.[4]

I had a strange feeling that evening, a premonition of coming ill. I walked down through the ranks of my silent or sleeping men, drawing a blanket more closely over one, and answering the broken murmurs of another, with a unreasoning yearning over them, thinking of what was before them, and wishing I could do what no mortal could do for them. Having passed all through the deep spreading ranks, I went to my quarters and dropped into an unaccustomed mood. A shadow seemed to brood over me, dark wings folding as it were [or a pall] and wrapping me in their embrace. Something said; "You will not be here again. This is your last." I had not the habit of taking a dark view of things; although for twenty seven days and nights together we had been under fire, more or less, never secure from danger for two hours together. I had a buoyant spirit — not light, and far from making light of things — but resolved and ready for my fate, meaning to face it, and not flinch. But this night, the premonition became oppressive, unbearable.[5]

---

4. A June 11 Field Return at the Library of Congress shows the aggregate of Chamberlain's 1st Brigade to be 97 officers and 2,071 men, not including those in the hospital or on detached duty. Petersburg, a city of almost 20,000 people before the war, was situated on the south bank of the Appomattox River, where it joins the James River, and is just twenty-three miles south of Richmond. It was a hub of roads and railroad lines that, as the territory north and east of Richmond was lost, became increasingly important to the survival of the Confederate capitol. In 1862, after the threat of General George McClellan's Peninsular Campaign to the region, a system of substantial fortifications around Petersburg was constructed that would become known as the Dimmock Line, finished in late 1863 and an arc of fortifications, studded with fifty-five batteries around the city. After Smith's June 15 attack breached a portion of the Dimmock Line, Confederates threw up a new defensive line of entrenchments, behind the position and designed to isolate their lost works. It became known as the Hagood Line, named after General Johnson Hagood who had chosen the position. By the night of June 17, the Rebels were again preparing a new line that would consolidate their forces by drawing them closer to the city. This third and final line of defense was laid out by Beauregard's chief engineer, Col. David B. Harris. In the early hours of June 18, the Rebels left bright fires burning and retired to their new line, working the rest of the night to throw up earthworks. It was the 5th Corps' misfortune that its attack on June 18 was made on the enemy's right, where much of the corps, including Chamberlain's 1st Brigade, was attacking the original Dimmock Line fortifications. Chamberlain's comment, that the orders issued the night of June 17 would send them the next morning against the "enemy's defensive works, now well strengthened and manned," bears the stamp of hindsight. On June 17 and during the morning of June 18, the works that Chamberlain's Brigade would attack at Rives' Salient were nearly bare of defenders. But ANV reinforcements poured into the beleaguered city during the night and morning of June 18. And by the time the 1st Brigade advanced against Rives' Salient that afternoon, the Rebel fortifications were fully manned. For details of the Confederate reinforcement of Petersburg on June 17 and 18, see paragraph #33 in the introduction. Rives' Salient took its name from its proximity to the farm of Timothy Rives [pronounced Reeves]. Rives, ironically, was known in the community for his Unionist sympathies. Nevertheless, he had been taken prisoner by Kautz's Cavalry during General Quincy Adams Gillmore's unsuccessful advance on the city earlier in June of 1864.

I went out to speak with some of my most intimate friends who were near. Among others I remember, Captain Twitchell, of the 7th Maine Battery Then to my own colonels; and finally to General Griffin. I bid them all a cheerful good evening, and went on to turn my greeting into a good bye. Most of them took it as ordinary exchange of courtesies; we had got used to sudden farewells, and fate too sudden for farewells; and I do not think much impression was left on any minds.[6]

But when I said to Griffin; "I feel like thanking you, General, for more kindnesses than I can recount tonight. I have appreciated them all; but have had no opportunity to speak to you about them before."

He looked up and said, "It seems to me this is a queer time for opportunities to pay compliments. We have other things to think of now. You are worn out. You had better turn in and go to sleep. We shall be awake early enough in the morning."

"General, this is my last night with you. You must let me thank you. I wish you to know my love for you".

"What do you mean," he sharply ejaculates — unwilling perhaps to let me see that he was moved.

"I shall fall tomorrow, General; this is my good bye:"

"Why do you think so?" he asks.

"The dark angel has said it to me".

"You have lost your poise. These terrible strains have been too much for you."

"No. General; I have perfect balance. You will see that. You will not be ashamed of me."

---

5. Though Chamberlain had made his way back to the army on the night of May 17-18, on May 20, he served on court-martial duty at 5th Corps headquarters. Rejoining his command the next day, for the next twenty seven days and nights he shared the movements of the 1st Division. At a Grand Army of the Republic (G.A.R.) "Smoker" many years later, Chamberlain would also recall, "I felt that I was going to be shot in the abdomen, and to guard against that bullet I strapped my blankets in front of my saddle instead of behind it as formerly."

6. Captain Adelbert Birge Twitchell was born in 1836 and graduated from Bowdoin Medical School's class of 1860. Twitchell first served as a lieutenant in the 7th Maine. By 1863, he was a captain in the 7th Maine Battery, which, at Petersburg in 1864, was serving with the 9th Corps. Brevetted a major in 1865, Twitchell survived the war to become a lumber merchant in New Jersey. Chamberlain's 1st Brigade, 1st Division, 5th Corps was actually mighty slim on "colonels." The former regiments of the 1st Corps, with the hard fighting they had seen with that corps and with the 5th, had been sadly deprived of line officers. The 121st Pennsylvania was commanded by Captain Nathaniel Lang. The 142nd Pennsylvania was under the command of Lt. Col. Horatio N. Warren. Maj. James Glenn had command of the 143rd Pennsylvania, and Lt. Col. John Irvin led the 149th Pennsylvania. Maj. George W. Jones commanded the 150th Pennsylvania, and the new 187th Pennsylvania was under the command of Lt. Col. Joseph F. Ramsey. Maj. Gen. Charles Griffin entered West Point in 1843. He graduated in 1847. He achieved the rank of major general and command of the 5th Corps in April of 1865.

"My God," he cries, "you are all wrong. I will tell you now what I was not going to. Warren and I have [been] talking things over. It is decided. You have done your full share of fighting. You are not to be put in tomorrow. You are held in reserve. So there."

"Yes, General; the reserve goes in when all is lost or must be saved by sacrifice. Let me lead tomorrow."

"Drop this; put away this feeling; we can't spare you, and I will not let you be exposed tomorrow."

"It will not be for you to say, General; Fate will cast the lot, or has cast it already."

"Oh, go to sleep; we will talk about this in the morning, if there is anything to talk about."

"Then, Good Night, General."[7]

Morning came with artillery at close range. The enemy knew we were of course preparing to attack their lines, and were using strong disuasives. All was astir in both lines — Restless, feverish, (it seemed to me knowing only my own front) — unplanned, tentative, or resting on contingencies.[8]

Soon our batteries were advanced to reply to those annoying us. The fire came back upon them fiercely. The enemy seemed now contemplating an attempt to take our guns by a dash.

---

7. Chamberlain, due to Griffin's confidence in him, had been given command of the 3rd Brigade of Griffin's 1st Division in late August of 1863 over the heads of several colonels senior to him. Forced to leave that command due to illness that November, Griffin did not assign permanent command of the 3rd Brigade to Bartlett until April 3, 1864. Griffin recommended promotion for Chamberlain to brigadier general of volunteers in the fall of 1863. He also endorsed a recommendation for his promotion on the day that Chamberlain took command of the new 1st Brigade in Griffin's division, in June of 1864. Regarding Chamberlain's statement of his love for Griffin, familiarity with nineteenth century correspondence prepares one for such expressions of love between friends. Theirs was a time when such expressions of affection could be and were made without raising today's suspicions regarding a homosexual relationship.

8. The Federal advance on the morning of June 18 did indeed become "unplanned, tentative, or resting on contingencies." During the night of June 17-18, Beauregard's force, having left a strong picket line at its front, retired to a hastily-prepared yet formidable new line in a strong position. Meade's army advanced through a heavy mist for a 4 a.m. attack. Elements of the 18th and 6th Corps, the 2nd Corps, the 9th Corps, and Crawford and Cutler's Division of the 5th Corps were positioned from right to left, respectively. There was a lingering, odd silence at the front before reports began coming in from all parts of the line that the enemy had retired. When the entire Federal line was ordered to continue its advance, it was discovered that a strong line of determined Rebel skirmishers must be fought and driven back before the enemy's new main line could be found. The AoP right soon pressed forward to the new Confederate entrenchments. On the left, however, the ground was broken by ravines and the Norfolk Railroad cut, deep and difficult to cross, and the Federal movement slowed and stalled. Elements of the 5th Corps that would be pushing westward over unknown ground to feel for the enemy's right flank would have to advance as much as one-and-one-half miles before reaching the enemy's

main line. On the 5th Corps' right, Crawford's Division maintained its position on the 9th Corps' left, slowly advancing with Burnside's men. Cutler, his 4th Division reinforced with the Maryland Brigade from General Romeyn Beck Ayres' Division, found that the Rebels had abandoned the Avery House on his front, and their trenches at the edge of the woods as well. Under his commanders' misapprehension that the Norfolk and Petersburg Railroad continued in a westerly direction, Cutler was ordered to advance with his left on the railroad. As soon as he appeared west of the Avery House, however, heavy fire from an advanced enemy rifled battery forced him from the open field. The entire 4th Division veered into the woods to the southwest for cover. Here, Cutler found the bridge across the deep railroad cut in flames, with enemy skirmishers on the opposite bank. While Cutler labored to rebuild the bridge and force a crossing, Ayres' 2nd Division was sent behind and to the left of Cutler to cover the 5th Corps' left flank. Griffin's 1st Division, Sweitzer's 2nd Brigade, Bartlett's 3rd Brigade, and Chamberlain's 1st Brigade, from right to left, respectively, advanced along the west side of the Norfolk Turnpike [also known as the Sussex or Baxter Road]. They moved to fill the gap developing between Crawford and Cutler. In this first action that his division would see at Petersburg, the aggressive Griffin pushed part of his force through Crawford's line in his impatience to gain his position. Many of the soldiers of Crawford's and Griffin's divisions who wrote of their experiences recalled with apparent horror this first advance on the morning of June 18. They were moving through the works that the men of Burnside's 9th Corps had captured and been driven from the previous evening. Many expressed the sentiment that, while descriptions of piles of dead were usually an exaggeration, in this case, it was all too true. It was a hard prelude to the fighting the men knew they must face that day. The 5th Corps advance continued. Sweitzer's Brigade, holding the right flank of the division, moved along the south side of the Norfolk Turnpike. And, while Bartlett's Brigade was held in reserve, it fell to the lot of Chamberlain's Brigade to move through a field of oats and into the open field beyond the Avery House. Though partly sheltered by a strip of pinewoods, at about 8 a.m., the men of the 1st Brigade formed their battle line under a severe slant fire from a battery the Rebels had posted on an outlying crest near the railroad. The enemy shells splintered the pines and solid shot bounded across the field.

The Avery House, though receiving heavy Rebel fire, became Warren's headquarters. Ironically, a number of large battlefield murals, undoubtedly depicting scenes from the Battle of Petersburg of 1781, covered the interior walls of the old dwelling.

NARA

Gen. Warren's 5th Corps headquarters at the Avery House

Then General Griffin rode up and said "We wish you would look out for these batteries here. They may try to take them."

"Certainly, General; they shall not take them," was the quiet assurance. He then rode away. I moved up close in rear of the guns, covering my men as I could by taking advantage of the ground. But the cannonading was sharp; the shot and shell tore up the whole ground in front of us. I had to ride along up & down the front of my men to reassure them; for many were falling, with no chance to strike back; and this is hard to bear. I knew that something different must be done, and soon; and was rather nervous myself. Then Griffin and Warren rode up to me; Griffin spoke: "It is too bad: I tried to prevent this; but those batteries out there must be dislodged   General Warren asks if you will do it."

"Does General Warren order this?" I asked. "I have a thought about it, and wish to know what the <u>orders</u> are."

"We do not order it; we wish it, if it is possible to be done. But it is a hard push up that open slope."

"That was what I was planning about, General; Will you let me do it in my own way? I think I can clear the batteries away — perhaps take them."

"Well, I am sorry for this; you will not think hard of me in any way?"

"I am thinking hard, but not of you", was the word as I rode up to my senior colonel and gave him orders to take the brigade to the left, not towards the enemy, but on parallel line somewhat sheltered from the enemy's fire, and mostly from their sight...and to gain a piece of woods on the right flank of the enemy's guns and wait for me.[9]

Then I turned and gave rein to my horse, and headed straight for the rebel batteries. I had seen something which looked not quite right, between us and the batteries; something I could not understand, looking, however, like a line of rifle pits for infantry, in front of their guns. I wished to see what this was, and there was no other way. I was not going to push

9. With Rebel artillery commanding Griffin's position in the open fields south of the Norfolk Road, the 1st Brigade's initial attempt to approach and cross the Norfolk Railroad was delayed, while its own artillery was brought up to support the attack. Mink's, Breck's, Cooper's and Anderson's Batteries, which had pushed forward with Cutler, occupied a ridge north of the woods where they directed their fire at the enemy across the railroad. And while Chamberlain's men were held in position, Captains Almont Barnes, John Bigelow, and Patrick Hart's batteries were brought up. Griffin undoubtedly hoped that his batteries could weaken or silence the Rebel artillery, but the Federal guns, in turn, needed the infantry's protection. Griffin's concern that the Rebels might make an attempt on his batteries was not misplaced. As the 1st Brigade was soon to discover, the Rebels already occupied the woods on their left. At about 10:30 a.m., Irvin, commander of 149th Pennsylvania and ranking colonel, led the 1st Brigade to the left as Chamberlain had ordered.

my brave men up to it, and possibly have them annihilated there. I was riding, of course, at headlong speed. Soon I was aware of a tearing Tartar overtaking me, and rushing up to my side.

"What in the name of Heaven are you going to do?" cries Griffin.

"I am just going to look at that strange ground there," was the reply, without checking speed.

"Then I am going with you," shouts Griffin. Meanwhile the Rebels seeing the strange embassy had begun to burst shell right over our heads and almost in our faces. We were aware that people from both armies were looking on, astonished, not knowing what circus-riding this was.

"There, you see, General, what I feared. I was not going to put my men up here." It was a deep railroad cut, and earth thrown up high as a man's breast just below the range of the enemy's artillery. Their shot would skim the crest and mow men down like reaping-machines. We both wheeled like a flash, with a half smile, strangely significant; he to his place with the center of his other brigades — I to my clump of woods, first taking a line to the rear before bearing to my [division's] left where my brigade was crossing the railroad track at level grade.[10]

We followed a rough track up to the woods, and there formed in two lines, with two regiments as a flanking force to support me on the left. I then instructed all the field officers what my plans were. We were to advance noiselessly as possible through the woods, and [on] emerging, fire there a volley & make a rush upon the flank of the rebel guns, and overwhelm them if possible before they could recover their wits. The second line was to follow the first at

---

10. At a G.A.R. "smoke talk" that Chamberlain attended in 1904, a reporter present quoted Chamberlain as saying that he rode out "to investigate a heap of red earth which appeared between the [Rebel] battery and the [1st Division's] main line." The Rebel skirmishers had turned the railroad cut that lay between their advanced battery and the approaching Federals into a formidable defensive line. They did so by throwing up dirt breast-high on the edge of the cut. It is interesting to consider that by this time [about 10:30 a.m.], though Warren, and likely Griffin, had been aware for some time that Cutler had encountered a railroad cut west of the Avery House, the 5th Corps was still feeling its way toward the Rebel right. But the curving of the cut from due west to due north as it passed through the 5th Corps front, placed that apparently hard-to-spot obstacle at varying distances from the advancing 5th Corps line. In his book *Passing of the Armies*, Chamberlain paid tribute to Griffin's apparently formidable riding abilities. Describing an event late in the day of the Battle of Five Forks, Chamberlain stated that Griffin "...dashed ahead of me and jumped his horse over the works. I thought myself a pretty good rider, but preferred a lower place in the breastworks." He also described his friend Griffin as "...ready for anything — a dash at the enemy with battery front, or [at] his best friend with a bit of satire when his keen sense of the incongruous or pretentious is struck...." It is possible that Chamberlain did not reach his brigade until all the men had already crossed to the south side of the railroad. While Chamberlain consistently describes their crossing as having taken place where the track reached level ground, one participant said the crossing took place over a bridge, muffled with grass.

a distance of 100 yards, till their line came to join with the first or replace it. It was a situation where the commander should lead; for quick action and change of action would be required. So with the whole staff, flag flying aloft, and the splendid lines close pressing, we made for the guns. Then a burst of artillery fire turned upon us with terrible effect. Down went my horse under me, a piece of case shot going through him; down went every one of my staff, wounded or unhorsed; down went my red Maltese cross, flag of our brigade; but on went everybody, on for the guns. Enfilading fire from great guns on our left, tore the earth before us, behind us, around us, through us; the batteries swung and gave us canister, & before we could reach them, limbered up and got off down the slope under cover of their main entrenchments. We only got their ground, and drove away the guns. I was mortified, greatly troubled. But the enfilading fire was so heavy we had to get a little below the crest we had carried, and prepare to hold it against attempts to recover it.[11]

---

11. The "rough track" to the left that the 1st Brigade traveled may have been the supply road which ran from Norfolk Road to the area of Battery No. 19 in the original Dimmock Line. Before entering the woods, around noon, Lt. Col. Warren, commander of the 149th Pennsylvania, recalled that Chamberlain assembled all of his regimental officers before this advance. While admitting that he was a stranger to them, Chamberlain stated that he was no stranger to their fighting abilities. While Lt. Col. Warren commented that this may have been "taffy," he observed that the talk "did us good, and without further investigation, we sent words to our men... that whatever might occur before night, we believed we had a `trump' as our brigade commander." Lt. Col. Warren wrote that the 121st, 143rd, 149th, and 150th Pennsylvania made up the front line, while the 187th and 142nd Pennsylvania, Chamberlain's safeguard for his left flank, followed in the second line. Warren described that, "...pushing forward we drove the enemy out of the woods into an open field, Col Com[man]d[in]g [Chamberlain] keeping his position about midway between the two lines, giving directions, when the rear line emerged from the woods, the Col observed his front line was not quite long enough and he sent an order to the officer commanding the 142nd to form on right of front line, then the column was moving forward briskly as they could and keep up a lively fire the 142nd made two flank movements under this fire on a fast double quick and formed on right of front line and opened fire, the line kept pushing forward until we had the enemy driven in to their last line of works..." A mile of open field fighting with the enemy's skirmishers ended with the escape of the Rebel batteries, much to Chamberlain's chagrin. The 1st Brigade not only received parting shots from the guns as they pulled out, but the brigade also came under heavy artillery fire from the salient on their front, Battery No. 25, and flanking fire from Battery No. 29 across the Jerusalem Plank Road. The Jerusalem Plank Road, so called because of the logs laid across the road to form a hard surface, ran between Petersburg and Jerusalem, now Courtland, Virginia. The latter advanced work, Fort Mahone, would earn the name "Fort Damnation" during the siege that followed. Seeking cover on the reverse slope of the ridge from which they had driven the enemy, by 1 p.m., the 1st Brigade was deployed squarely in front of and some 300 yards away from Battery No. 25. This area, known as Rives' Salient, was the point at which the new Rebel line joined the formidable fortifications of the original Dimmock Line. [Chamberlain's position was roughly one-third of a mile forward of the area where Fort Sedgwick would be constructed during the ensuing siege. This said fort soon earned the name "Fort Hell."] Thus, the 1st Brigade's fate was the same as that of the units to its left, Cutler's 4th Division and Ayres' 2nd Division. They had the unenviable positions as the only AoP attackers on June 18 that assaulted the formidable works the Rebels had completed in 1863. And, by the time Chamberlain, Cutler, and Ayres made their mid-afternoon attack on the Rebel fortification, the enemy's parapets and artillery were fully manned by newly arrived elements of the ANV. Chamberlain's 1st Brigade flag was a white triangular banner featuring a red Maltese Cross.

Pondering and studying the situation, I saw that we could use artillery to advantage. I sent back to Griffin or Warren, a mile, I should think — for some artillery, meanwhile setting my pioneers to digging platforms just under the crest of the hill, making level ground for the guns to be worked on when they should arrive. Before long, up came Bigelow with the 9th Massachusetts, and Hart of the 15th New York, followed by another, Barnes' 1st New York. Mink was across the [railroad] cut firing in[to] the Ice House to my right front. We helped the guns up into the places I had made for them, laying their muzzles in the grass close to the earth, so that nobody could suspect we had artillery there. We were so far advanced from the rest of the army that I did not quite like to give the enemy a chance to study up plans to capture our exposed guns; but I put two good regiments, the 150th [Pa], and [?] regiments, to guard the exposed left flank, and busied myself in strengthening our position.[12]

---

12. It was possible for Chamberlain to send back directly to his division commander for artillery, for during the reorganization of the 5th Corps on June 5, Warren had assigned three batteries each to the 1st and 2nd Divisions, while creating a six battery reserve artillery for the corps. While this facilitated the quicker movement of batteries, it offended Wainwright, the talented, but outspoken 5th Corps' chief of artillery, who blamed this decision on Griffin's influence with General Warren. A possible explanation for why control of Wainwright's batteries had been wrested away from him can be found in the artillery commander's own diary prior to the reorganization. It holds a number of examples of the confrontations Wainwright had with Warren and Griffin over the placement of batteries. In his diary, Wainwright was particularly unabashed in his expressions of dislike and disdain for Griffin. Interestingly, Wainwright's is the only criticism of Griffin's well-known artillery expertise that this writer has encountered. Bigelow, Barnes, and Hart are the battery commanders that came to the 1st Brigade's assistance. Regarding the position of supporting troops, in his "Reminiscences..." Chamberlain stated, "We were a mile away from the rest of the army, and I prepared to `take care of myself.'" It is unclear whether Chamberlain, by "we," was speaking of just the 1st Brigade, or also of Cutler's and Ayres' Divisions, all of which alone confronted a portion of the original Dimmock Line. They were all isolated from the rest of the AoP, which at its nearest was a mile to the north. And between these elements of the 5th Corps and the remainder of the AoP intervened the Norfolk and Petersburg Railroad. This was a significant obstacle to any possibility of sending reserves to assist these isolated units of the 5th Corps. At midday, as Chamberlain's 1st Brigade placed its batteries and dug in, Cutler's 4th Division had taken up a position in the woods near the Jerusalem Plank Road, no less than three-fourths of a mile to the rear and left of the 1st Brigade. Ayres' Division, meanwhile, continued to force its way west to meet what seemed to be an increasing threat to the 5th Corps' left. The division had become pinned down under heavy enemy fire in a position confronting the Dimmock Line to the left of Cutler. It is likely that Chamberlain was more concerned about receiving support on his left than his right, perhaps because the ground to the right of his front was cut by the gullies and runs of Taylor Branch or Poor Creek [sometimes referred to by the Federals as "Poo" Creek], making an enemy attack from that direction less likely. But regardless of the chances of enemy incursion from that direction, on Chamberlain's right there was essentially no support. Though General Warren reported at noon that both wings of the 5th Corps had connected, Sweitzer's 2nd Brigade, advancing with supporting batteries, had shifted to near the Norfolk Road as it advanced on the left of Crawford's Division. While Chamberlain's Brigade had advanced to drive off Rebel artillery and take a position behind the ridge from which they drove them, the 2nd Brigade took the railroad cut in their front and assumed a position in the ravine in front of the Rebel main line. This was located about one-fourth mile beyond the railroad. Thus, Sweitzer was well over a mile from Chamberlain's right, and with Sweitzer and Cutler so far from Chamberlain's position, it is hardly surprising that Chamberlain, as he confronted Rives' Salient, felt he was, indeed, on his own.

In the midst of this, a staff-officer came out, much excited with his difficult journey, and gave me the order: "The General commanding, (he did not say which general, but it was either Meade or Grant; it was not an officer I had seen before), desires you to attack and carry the works in your front."

"Does the General know where I am?" I asked. "Let me show you! They are the interior works, the main works at Petersburg, and am I to attack alone?"

"I gave you the order", he says, "that is all I have to say."

"Very well, Colonel, you are Colonel ########### are you not?"

"I am, sir."

"Will you kindly take a written message from me to the General?"

"Certainly, if you wish; I see that there may be occasion for it."

"There is," I said.[13]

And I took out my field-book and wrote as follows: "I have received the order to assault the enemy's main works in my front. The General commanding cannot possibly be aware of the situation here. From where I write this I can count ten or twelve pieces of artillery behind earthworks, so placed as to give me a cross-fire, and a line of works with not less than 5,000 infantry, easily sweeping the slope down which I must advance, not less than 300 yards from this point. A large Fort is on my left and perfectly enfilades with heavy guns the whole slope in my front. It will be only slaughter for men to charge upon this front, unsupported. Fully aware of the responsibility I assume, my duty to

---

13. When Chamberlain wrote "The Charge at Fort Hell" in 1899, apparently he hadn't been able to discover whether his order to attack at Rives' Salient had originated with Grant or Meade. In his "Reminiscences" written in 1903, Chamberlain seems to be attributing the order to Grant, but all evidence indicates that on June 17 and 18 at Petersburg, Meade was completely in charge of the AoP except for the elements of the 6th Corps with Butler. Nor did Chamberlain ever identify the staff officer who brought him the orders, and the above seems to indicate that he chose not to name this officer, whose conduct might be considered less than wise or admirable. A news writer reported that Chamberlain stated in 1904 that the officer was a lieutenant colonel. Chamberlain biographer Alice Trulock hypothesized that it might have been Lt. Col. Theodore Lyman, one of Meade's staff officers who had indeed been sent to the 5th Corps early that morning, and communicated with Meade throughout the day. But Lyman, who wrote detailed accounts of his activities, especially when he was sent on hazardous duty, records spending the day with General Warren, making no mention of having gone on such a dangerous errand to the 1st Brigade that day. Comstock, Grant's A.D.C., also spent the entire day of June 18 moving from place to place along the AoP front, but there is no evidence one way or the other that he gave or carried orders to Chamberlain.

my veteran soldiers compels me to ask to postpone this charge until the General can be informed of the circumstances. In my opinion, if an assault is to be made, it should be by not less than the whole Army of the Potomac." I thought it likely that it was not known at head quarters that I had carried this crest. The order might have meant this [crest].[14]

No sooner had this hasty message left my control than I began to reflect on the presumptuous character of giving my unasked opinion about the assault. I was not commanding the Army of the Potomac, and my last remark was uncalled for and highly censurable. Whatever might be said of an officer, in any manner refusing to attack the enemy when ordered to do so, this pert advice about the Army of the Potomac being the only proper agent of an assault was unpardonable. How I could have been such a fool, passed my understanding, & [I thought] my premonition about this being my last day in the field would soon be realized. I expected nothing less than an "arrest" and an order to the rear for charges of the most serious kind known to the service. I began to think what influence I could bring to bear upon the President, through Pitt Fessenden, Henry Wilson, Charles Sumner, and Lot Morrill, to secure a pardon before sentence. I called my Colonels up and told them I expected soon to be taken away. I did not tell them how. I gave them however my general ideas of the situation, and of the best manner of making an assault when ordered. It is needless to say that I was in a very distressed state of mind — shame above all, taking the

---

14. A letter reproduced in a newspaper article [*Lewiston Journal*, September 1-6, 1900] and represented as a copy of the letter Chamberlain sent in reply to the initial order to attack, would indicate that this version paraphrases his response. See Appendix C for transcription of Chamberlain's response. Many years later, Chamberlain, accompanied by a knowledgeable guide and armed with an old worn Confederate war map from the period of the battle, revisited that part of the line known as Rives' Salient. Chamberlain confirmed that there had been five guns in the redan on their front; while the two lunettes on either side had seven guns each; and behind the interval, in a retired work, four guns, for a total of twenty-three guns opposite their advance. Four hundred yards to the 1st Brigade's left stood Fort Mahone, its seven guns enfilading every inch of Chamberlain's attack. Beauregard first posted Kershaw's [General Lafayette McLaws'] Division "a cheval" on Jerusalem Plank Road in support of General Henry Alexander Wise's men. As Kershaw relieved Wise's men, his right rested on the Jerusalem Plank Road, his line extended with the works across an open field and bent back toward the front of the [Blandford] cemetery. General Field's [General John Bell Hood's] Division took up its position on Kershaw's right. The Texas Brigade, posted on Field's left, connected with Kershaw's right at a place "to the south of Blanford [sic] Cemetery on the lower slope of the hill." Field's right rested near the Weldon Railroad. Many years after the war, a news reporter would attribute to Chamberlain the comment that the unsupported attack the 1st Brigade was asked to make upon Rives' Salient was "desperate, hopeless and useless."

"pith" all out of me. In about half an hour I saw the same staff-officer coming up the rear slope of the crest. I was ready to give up my sword. I was a pitiful thing — I worn thin, burnt brown, taxed and tasked beyond my powers by severe service. I had unflinchingly and uncomplainingly rendered, and having just achieved a good piece of work for which I knew I deserved praise — to be seen disarmed, disgraced, sneaking to the rear, with not even the dignity of a lamb led to the slaughter, but more like a dog kicked away from decent company. (It never occurred to me — not having the opportunity to secure counsel, to plead insanity.) [15]

[I was] in the lowest pit of dejection, [as] the staff-officer approached.

"Yes, Sir, I am ready," was my first word, spoken before he came to a stand.

"The General says you are quite right in what you say about the assault. The whole army will attack." I felt as if I were on wings. Life, death, had no terrors.

"But," and here came in the balancer, the "twist" pretty fairly getting even with me for my pertness, "from the position of things, you being advanced as you are, it will be necessary to guide on you. You will be the 'battalion of direction.' The General wishes to know the precise minute when you will be ready to attack."

"Now!" I greedily answered, glad to gulp down any medicine, as a punishment for that sin of foolishness, for which no provision seems to be made in the [economies] of nature or grace.

"Oh, no," he responds, "that will not give time to get the order to all the commands. But we want an hour fixed, for simult[an]eous movement."

"Very well, sir, how much time will it take?"

"Perhaps an hour," he replies.

I took out my watch, and compared it with his; "I will attack at 3 o'clock, precisely" was my final word. [16]

---

15. William Pitt Fessenden, former U.S. representative and senator from Maine, was chairman of the Senate Committee on Finance during the first years of the Civil War, and served as Lincoln's secretary of the Treasury, 1864-1865. Henry Wilson was an influential U.S. senator from Massachusetts, and chairman of the Senate Military Committee during the war. Charles Sumner, one of the founders of the Free Soil Party, was a powerful U.S. senator from Massachusetts, 1851-1874. Lot Morrill, served as U.S. senator from Maine, 1861-1876. Though Chamberlain's apprehension regarding the repercussions of having questioned his orders was genuine, there is a good deal of "tongue-in-cheek" in his manner of relating it. While it is likely that Chamberlain had met Secretary Fessenden, and perhaps had been introduced to Senator Morrill, there is no evidence that he was well acquainted with any of these influential gentlemen in 1864.

16. Patrick DeLacy, a sergeant with the 143rd Pennsylvania, wrote after the war that he was in earshot of Chamberlain when the staff officer returned with orders for a coordinated attack. DeLacy remembered Chamberlain stating, "I will take care of my front but want my flanks protected." The staff officer informed Chamberlain that Cutler's 4th Division had orders to support the 1st Brigade's left. Chamberlain went back to see Cutler to relate his own orders and the information he had been given, that Cutler was to support him. Chamberlain commented on the advance that, "...I regarded it as a desperate attempt but I was going into it with all my might, & I asked him to move in echelon with me or to divert the fire of the fort on our left front so that I should not be mown down like grass." Chamberlain also related Cutler's reaction. "He seemed amazed. `I do not take orders from you,' he says. `I am your senior, you had rather take orders from me.'"

Chamberlain responded, "I have orders General & I suppose you have yours. We are to work together, & I think it well we should have an understanding."

Cutler retorted, "I shall know what to do when the time comes."

Chamberlain would later observe, "But it seems the time doesn't `come,' He didn't anyway."

Cutler, meanwhile reported his position to 5th Corps headquarters as about 600 yards from the Rebel works, and he stated that he had received a blank piece of paper instead of an order. In a statement that defies explanation, Cutler added that Chamberlain "understands that he was to take the crest where I am." Details of Chamberlain's confrontation with Cutler and that commander's subsequent failure to support the 1st Brigade are found in a fragment of what is apparently a private letter from Chamberlain to an unknown correspondent. Chamberlain makes no reference to Cutler's behavior in any of his Petersburg accounts or addresses. Cutler [1807-1866], served as colonel of the 6th Wisconsin and with several brigades of the old 1st Corps, seeing much hard service. In the spring of 1864, Cutler ascended to command of the 4th Division, 5th Corps, after the death of General James Wadsworth at the Wilderness. The division had endured rough handling by the enemy at the Wilderness and at the North Anna, and by late May of 1864, Wainwright described Cutler as "very much broken." Though a brave man, Cutler was known for being gruff and touchy about matters of rank. It was Chamberlain's misfortune that Cutler was still bitter that the veteran regiments that made up Chamberlain's new 1st brigade had been taken from Cutler's division. Regarding the source of Chamberlain's orders, the instructions that Chamberlain received from this unidentified staff officer to delay his attack until orders could be issued for a coordinated attack, add to the mystery of their source. It seems unlikely that the orders came from Meade. Having exploded with impatience at the delays that his corps commanders encountered when trying to gain position for a simultaneous attack, Meade would eventually insist that all his corps commanders attack immediately without reference to the support on their flanks. Meanwhile, no orders for a mid-afternoon attack apparently reached the 2nd Brigade on Chamberlain's right, for after their morning advance, there is no evidence that they advanced again until 6 p.m. that evening. Seemingly oblivious to having failed to support Chamberlain's 3 p.m. attack, a regimental history blames the 1st Brigade for the 2nd Brigade's failure to take the enemy line, citing Chamberlain and the 1st Brigade's failure to advance with them during their 6 p.m. attack. But, it should also be noted that Sweitzer sent his 2nd Brigade in at less than full strength, holding three of his regiments in reserve.

In preparation for the 1st Brigade's 3 p.m. advance, Lt. Col. Warren, in command of the 142nd Pennsylvania at the time, would recall that Chamberlain summoned his regimental commanders. Once they were informed of the attack, they were told that their lines would remain as they were, with the veteran regiments in the front line, and the 187th in their rear for support. Chamberlain would take up a position at the center half way between the two lines. The regiments were told to make as much noise as they could. They were to go as fast as possible through the ravine in their front in any kind of order, but present a solid front when they climbed to the top of the other side. They were to push forward without firing a shot and mount the enemy's works. But Lt. Col. Warren remembered that Chamberlain also warned them, before uncovering from the ledge of the ravine near the Rebel works "to cast our eyes right and left and if the brigades on either or both sides broke and retreated... to be cautious about going in, as we might be captured." Lt. Col. Warren would later comment, "My motive in giving this account is to show how much better Americans fight when their officers explain to them the object of the Orders issued, and the manner in which they desire them carried out." Warren also said, "In the 23 general engagements my regiment was in, we were never in a more desperate situation and in my opinion never fought so well, because they fought intelligently the entire credit of which is due to Col. Chamberlain for whom ever after the men and officers entertained an undying regard." Maj. M. L. Blair of the 143rd Pennsylvania, on the right of the 1st Brigade line, would recall, "While lying prone on the ground... Col. J. L. Chamberlain... stepped leisurely along our front and said kindly to us: `Comrades, we have now before us a great duty for our country to perform, and who knows but the way in which we acquit ourselves in this perilous undertaking may depend the ultimate success of the preservations of our grand republic. We know that some must fall, it may be any of you or I; But I feel that you will all go in manfully and make such a record as will make all our loyal American people forever grateful. I can but feel that our action in this crisis is momentous, and who can know but in the providence of God our action today may be the one thing needful to break and destroy this unholy rebellion.'" These words, Blair declared, "put new life and determination into this tired and battered brigade..."

LOC
Gen. Lysander Cutler

LOC
Col. Jacob Sweitzer

No more dejection now. It was projection. And lively at that. The artillery had meanwhile been getting up and into the platforms I had partly prepared. This suited me well. The muzzles would be laid right in the short grass on the crest when pushed into action, but were protected when loading after the recoil. I went along the rear of the guns advising with the commanding officer about getting a slant fire on the enemy's guns in the works before and slightly below us, so as to knock them off of their trunnions if possible, and be ready to give case shot or canister when demonstrations of the enemy should offer good effects. My chief solicitude was lest this fire which I directed to open only when my men were well down in front below the line of their fire, should demoralize or injure my men, by the stripping lead of the band of shell or too premature bursting of case shot above their heads. I also gave particular instructions to my colonels, especially to the two senior colonels likely to succeed me. I did not conceal from them my expectation of not long surviving; for I resolved to lead the charge in person. I held my watch in hand, and when the minute hand was on the mark for 3 o'clock, I told the bugler to sound the 'charge.'[17]

Up rose my brave men; past the batteries they press; closing in in front of them; down the slope they go; muskets on the shoulder; bayonets fixed; for I had instructed on no account to commence firing in front of the enemy's works, this would distract their attention from the main purpose, which was to go over the works, and taking them any way hand to hand. As I had determined, I led the movement with my whole staff, dismounted — the horses had all gone down under the fierce fire we encountered in carrying the crest at first. I had a color-bearer following me, also on foot. At this outburst of men after a moment's astonishment, the enemy opened with every kind of missile man has invented. My men being below the line of fire of our own artillery, this began too, with whatever it could best use — solid shot, first, shell short-fused — the distance was from 200 yards to 400 according to objects needing engagement — and what I dreaded, case-shot — from which some explosions troubled my men — or possibly, the stripping lead and sabots. Now rose such a fury of fire as never was concentrated on one small space before; crowned by the heavy fire of Fort Mahone on our left, which as soon as we got fairly in front of our own guns had perfect enfilading range, & used it "well" — in their estimation, no doubt.[18]

---

17. Mink's Battery H of the 1st New York Light Artillery threw up lunettes and took position on the right of 5th Corps nearly opposite the reservoir, and fired into the Rebel works near an icehouse on the right of Chamberlain's front. It had been Mink's battery that Wainwright credited with saving the 5th Corps' right on May 23, 1864, when Cutler's 4th Division broke at the North Anna. The batteries in the 1st Brigade's rear were Bigelow's 9th Massachusetts, Hart's 15th New York, and Barnes' 1st New York. These batteries would be shoved up onto the crest, and, when Chamberlain gave the signal, they were to open on the enemy's works as soon as the men of the 1st Brigade had passed down into the ravine in their front. Chamberlain did indeed worry about "demonstrations of the enemy." He was pleased that the crest offered some protection for the batteries, though the crews still suffered from the enemy's artillery and musket fire. Chamberlain was fully aware, however, that if the enemy staged an attack to take the guns, the batteries would find it difficult to withdraw. His worry that his own troops would suffer from their own batteries' fire also proved justified. Several 1st Brigade accounts describe that their own batteries dropped shots in the midst of their regiments. Chamberlain's senior colonels were Lt. Col. Warren, commander of the 142nd Pennsylvania, and Lt. Col. Irvin, commander of the 149th Pennsylvania, with Irvin being senior officer. Of Chamberlain's timing of the attack, Captain Ranford B. Webb of the 187th Pennsylvania would later write, "The Colonel came down the rear of our line... took out his watch and held it in his hand, still looking to the rear - it might have been five minutes, to me it was a lifetime. He stepped between Companies "D" and "I" and several paces to the front, faced about, drew his sword, and gave the command clear as a trumpet, 'Attention! Trail arms! Double quick, march!' And waving his sword toward the fort on our right, he set us the pace forward. My nightmare was gone. I had received an inspiration like an electric shock. I must do as my leader had done — I could not help it. Comrade Ployer says that I also waved my sword toward the fort... and shouted... 'Come on.' If it was a brave act, give Colonel Chamberlain the credit for it. I thought he had challenged me to a foot race."

18. Some seventeen years after the battle, Chamberlain, on visiting and finding the area of his brigade's advance on Rives' Salient, described, "...I looked down & saw a bullet & while stooping to pick it up, another & another appeared in sight & I took up six within as many feet of each other and of the spot where I fell. You may imagine what the havoc must have been that day. And for 17 years relic hunters have been carrying away lead & iron from the field — amounting, I was told, to cart-loads. I could easily no doubt have found many more had I searched, or kicked away the earth a little — But these I have, & that other that made so straight a way through me, will do." The handful of bullets and balls, as well as the minié ball that severely wounded Chamberlain, are all at the Pejepscot Historical Society's Chamberlain Museum in Brunswick, Maine. To add to the 1st Brigade's troubles, several unit accounts report that they received casualties from the firing of their own artillery. One artillery account also reports that when the infantrymen began coming back after their failed attack, they were followed by the enemy, and artillery continued to fire through friend and foe.

I had formed two lines three regiments in the front line and the 187th in the second, a "new" regiment, full ranks, and stout hearts; with two regiments skilled marksmen as a special column on the left to guard that exposed flank in whatever way should be necessary. This now seems to me not the best formation; for it gave my new regiment the awful spectacle of the havoc made in my first line; my reason for this was, however, that none but experienced soldiers should try to go over works with the bayonet. And the two gallant regiments I had placed in column, (they were small in numbers) on the left, were a good — bad — mark for all the demons that had [them] at their mercy, front and flank. But I had thought it necessary to guard strongly that unsupported flank, especially as an attempt would be made I thought it likely, to capture my artillery, which had no chance to get out except right in the face of some batteries now disclosed on my left. A very exposed, and dangerous position for them, unless strongly supported, which I saw, from my advanced ground when clear of the crest, had utterly failed to make effective demonstration. I cannot say there was any "surprise" anywhere; I had perfectly comprehended all that happened, before I moved a step, and had so told the staff-officer bringing me the orders. For some reason I do not now feel able to state I had no confidence that the expected "support" promised me would amount to any thing. It proved true; that was all. So I do not know that I was at fault in my dispositions, however severely they exposed my command. My main business was to take the works in front. What kind of a situation we should be in then, with Mahone pouring its great shot down on us, unless the miracle should be wrought of our other troops carrying or silencing it, I hardly charged myself with thinking; that was for my superiors, "commanding the Army of the Potomac."[19]

In five minutes' time my flag-bearer was shot dead. I took the flag from his dying hands, without a look at the poor fellow, and pressed on. My staff were being disabled — some with wounds, some sent to watch or help the various points of greatest danger, especially my left. The very earth was plowed and torn to pieces by the shot directed at my troops, a clear mark on the side hill for the whole force of the enemy from every quarter. The great shot from the fort on the left sent the turf and stones through our ranks, filling the air with tornado debris. The musketry was like a boiling sea. Suddenly I found myself on the borders of a marsh or bog, which men could not well pass. This must not catch my men, I thought, and made a half face to the left and gave the command, "Incline to the left. To the left." Nobody could hear a word — any more than at the bottom of Hell. I raised the flag, the red Cross, high as I could and waving this in one hand and my saber with the other towards the left, continued shouting and signaling, "To the left. To the left."[20]

In the hiss and roar and blinding, flying earth, standing and so signaling I felt a sharp hot flush that seemed to cut the spinal marrow out of my back-bone. A twelve-pound shell or case-shot had exploded right behind me as I was faced, and the pieces came thrumming by my ears. My thought

---

19. In paragraph #12 of "The Charge at Fort Hell," Chamberlain named the 150th Pennsylvania as one of the regiments he sent to protect the brigade's left flank and the artillery.

Of the support that "utterly failed to make effective demonstration," 4th Division commander, Cutler, would later report that he did not receive the order to advance until almost 3 p.m., at which time he formed his brigade in the woods more than half a mile from the enemy works. Various reports indicate that the 4th Division's advance may have begun twenty to thirty minutes later than that made by Chamberlain's 1st Brigade at 3 p.m. Col. J. W. Hoffman's 2nd Brigade, on the 4th Division's right, reported making a spirited advance until it approached the ravine in its front. Under a terrible fire from the front and both flanks, most of the brigade broke and retired. About 200 men passed through the ravine in their front, only to become pinned to the ground on the opposite side. The historian of the 24th Michigan bitterly recalled that after coming under as severe a fire as they had ever experienced, Cutler, wishing to bring his second line directly behind his first line, ordered the Iron Brigade to move by the right flank. This had the effect of changing their formation to one which exposed four rather than two ranks deep to the fire of the enemy. Once the survivors of this maneuver reached the protection of a hill on the right, few obeyed the order to advance again. Wainwright, the 5th Corps' chief of artillery, found several hundred men of the 4th Division near his guns. Attempting to rally them and take them forward, only a few dozen seemed prepared to advance with him. Wainwright confessed that had he been able to persuade more men to follow him into another attack, it was likely he would not have lived to tell about it. Cutler, also suffered from lack of support on his flank, for on his left, Ayres' Division failed to advance. Ayres' front was swept by Rebel fire, and Cutler also believed that Ayres had not received the order in time for the 3 p.m. attack. Neither Cutler nor Ayres would deliver the saving miracle of silencing Fort Mahone. DeLacy of the 143rd Pennsylvania offered testimony of having seen the brigade on his left break and retire, likely Hoffman's Brigade, 4th Division. Lt. Col. Warren offers that the brigades on the left and right broke, a puzzling observation, for it seems that the brigade on the right did not attack at 3 p.m. [See annotation #16 for evidence that Sweitzer's Brigade did not advance until several hours after Chamberlain's attack.]

20. DeLacy of the 143rd Pennsylvania would initially describe the first line's advance as a quick march, soon double quick, finally on the run. DeLacy's account is at odds with Lt. Col. Warren's description of Chamberlain. Warren said Chamberlain maintained a position between the first and second lines. DeLacy remembered Chamberlain in front of the first line carrying the brigade flag, a statement which seems to agree with Chamberlain's statements in paragraph #18 and #21 of "The Charge at Fort Hell." DeLacy described the swampy ravine as being filled with brush, running sweet briars and alders with part of the ground marshy with deep mud, and in some places the brush and swamp was forty to fifty-feet wide. Beyond it was a stream between four to six-feet in width, which ran across their front, its banks perpendicular, from three to five-feet deep. As previously mentioned, Federal maps give this stream the outlandish name of Poo Creek, an inadvertent abbreviation of its real name, Poor Creek, also known as Taylor's Creek.

was that I had been shot in the back — in the middle of the back, below the belt. This was all I could think of for a moment, and the shame of it was worse than death. To be shot in the back, in the face of the enemy! This was worse than refusing to attack. I was lost, dead or alive, and better dead! I had not fallen. That was strange for the blow was strong. But I was well braced as I stood waving my two emblems of command; and braced also in mind, had not fallen. Perforce I dropped flag-staff and saber to the ground; holding them upright, however, without claiming much heroism for that, as I had need of both for my staff and stand. But I put on an extreme straightness of posture, wishing to countervail the appearance of cowardly turning my back to the enemy and getting proof of it in the telling shot. It never occurred to me that an officer leading his men in a charge might properly have to face aside to give effect to a command. I remember and always shall, the looks on the faces of my men as they came up to me in line — dear, brave fellows — their writhing line stiff and strong as the links of a chain-cable, as they broke file [and] gave way to the left "to pass obstacle." A minute has not passed, when as I turned to look sharply at my second line, my noble new regiment coming up so grandly into this terrible test...[21]

I felt in my sword hand a gush of hot blood. I looked down then for the first time. I saw the blood spurting out of my right hip-side, and saw that it had already filled my long cavalry boots to overflowing, and also my baggy reinforced trousers, and was running out at both pocket welts. Not shot in

---

21. For further description of Chamberlain's first thoughts when he was shot, see appendix A. Chamberlain clearly indicates that he had been leading his first line rather than the second line, for he describes that first line breaking files to pass him, before he turned to watch his second line coming on. Lt. West Funk of the 121st Pennsylvania and a member of Chamberlain's staff, also describes Chamberlain as leading the first line. Chamberlain had apparently feared that his men would think him unwilling to go on with them, for in this account he initially wrote but crossed out, "...as they broke files [&] gave way 'to pass obstacle.' I fancied I could see the sorry but half-forgiving look as they thought I was showing the white feather — letting them pass me to the terrible front out of which came even now bellowing and bursts and spitting lead and hurtling iron." Chamberlain commented in 1900 that, to that day, he vividly remembered the expressions on the faces of his men as they swept past him while he was standing rigidly erect as if inspecting them. It should be noted that Chamberlain's testimony supports the historian of the 187th's assertion that a portion of their regiment reached and passed through the ravine to the ground beyond. It was an accomplishment that Lt. Col. Warren of the 142nd denied them, though he explained that the 187th Pennsylvania failed to come up because it had been cut to pieces. DeLacy perhaps provides an explanation for the discrepancy, when he states that the 187th Pennsylvania broke and recoiled under terrible fire, but "to the everlasting credit of the officers and men they were rallied and brought back under the same galling fire, which accounts for the fearful loss of that regiment, but it spoiled the effect of the main charge." DeLacy went on to describe the old regiments as clinging to their advanced positions with great tenacity, while the 187th was brought up on their right.

the back then! I do not think I was ever so happy in my life. My first thought was of my Mother, my Huguenot-blooded mother; how glad she would be that her boy was not shot in the back! "Had he his wounds before?" Then it is well. I found that I had been shot through by a minié ball — the round hole was plain — from hip joint to hip joint — from right to left, just in front of the joints.[22]

I was already faint with loss of blood. I sank first to my knees, then leaning on my right elbow. One of my staff ran up now — Major Funk — and fell distracted with grief on my very body, begging me to let him go for a surgeon, or have me taken to one. I knew either to be impossible, and useless. "No", I said, "my dear fellow; there is much better for you to do on this field. I saw a

---

22. The bullet that entered on the right did not exit on the left. The ball, according to Chamberlain's description in paragraph #25, lodged just behind his left hip (not in front of the joint as Chamberlain describes above), remaining just below the skin. But recent research by urologist Dr. George Files suggests that a fragment of the bullet or bone exited on the left and caused the bleeding at Chamberlain's left hip. Chamberlain's mother, Sarah Brastow Chamberlain, was the daughter of Billings and Lydia (Dupee) Brastow. Her mother was a descendent of Jean Dupuis, who was born about 1660 in La Rochelle, France, and immigrated to Boston, Massachusetts, in 1685. Mother Chamberlain's grandfather, Charles Dupuis, served in the army during the American Revolution, at which time the spelling of his name was changed in an army list to Dupee.

Brewer Public Library

Sarah Brastow Chamberlain

movement from the enemy's lines just as I was struck, to take the batteries on the crest. Run to the 150th Pennsylvania and tell them to take care of those guns at all events. And tell Bigelow or Hart to prepare to give canister in his front, but look for our men and not fire into them. We will take care of his left flank." Then came up Major Osborne Jones, inspector on my staff — agonized. "Tell Colonel [Irvin] that he is in command of the brigade," I said. "The assault is checked; I can see that. Get the men where they will not be destroyed. Don't let them try to stand here under this fire. Either over, or out!" I would not let him try to get me away. It would not be worth the cost. I could see that my assault had failed, and that a counter-charge was preparing; men were already coming over their works beyond our left, and forming for attack. This must be attended to. That was my chief thought.[23]

---

23. Funk of the 121st Pennsylvania would later write that he and Lt. Benjamin F. Walters of the 143rd Pennsylvnia, who was also serving on Chamberlain's staff, carried their commander from the field, and later to the hospital. But in several accounts, including this one, Chamberlain confirms that credit for removing him from the field should be given to Bigelow's men of the 9th Massachusetts Battery. Bigelow, sweeping the field in his front with his field glasses, caught sight of Chamberlain's shoulder straps and sent four of his men with a stretcher to take him off. A letter from Bigelow to Chamberlain also confirms his men's rescue mission. Chamberlain relinquished command to senior officer Irvin of the 149th Pennsylvania. Though the promised support for the 1st Brigade's flanks had failed to materialize, after passing their stricken commander, the men of the 1st Brigade pressed on toward the Rebel fortification. The unit history of the 121st Pennsylvania describes the regiment as advancing as far as the ravine or stream bed, where it remained under fire from both the Rebels and its own artillery. Lt. Col. Warren tells that upon realizing that the brigades on either side had not come up in support, it was difficult to prevent the 142nd Pennsylvania from going over the enemy works. Hugging the side of the ravine to escape the canister fire from Fort Mahone, Warren soon had his men digging rifle pits. DeLacy of the 143rd related that while the marshy area and bushes of the ravine proved difficult to get through, the stream itself presented a real obstacle. "Many of the boys jumped across it and fell back into the mud & water..." By the time they clambered up the steep sides of Poor Creek and gained the field near the enemy's works, they witnessed Cutler's force off to their left and rear breaking and retiring. Meanwhile, much of the ardor of 149th Pennsylvania's assault was lost when the enemy's canister hit them. But, while some the regiment dropped back behind the crest they had started from, part of the 149th reached the next ridge. The history of the 150th tells that the men worked their way to within fifty yards of the Rebel works, but their line had been so thinned by enemy fire, that they were too weak for the final rush.

A sergeant of the 150th remembers that recall was finally sounded, the regiment falling back to the crest from which it started in order to protect the brigade's left flank and the artillery. The 187th Pennsylvania claimed to have advanced to the base of the slope leading up to the Rebel works before the withering fire forced it back. By 4 p.m., the 187th Pennsylvania was back to the position it had started from, but without 180 of its members, who were dead or wounded on the field. Artillery commander Wainwright stated that when the enemy followed retreating Federals in, he ordered his guns to keep firing "even through our own runaways." A good many of the 1st Brigade had made their way off the field by 5 p.m., while those still pinned by enemy fire in front of the enemy works had to wait until dark to make the hazardous journey to the rear. The men who had made their way to the rear were greeted with the news that they were going in again. It was enough to make the men of the 187th Pennsylvania pin their names on their coats. The hour for another advance would come and go before the waiting men received word that there would be no more attacks. As for the threat of an enemy counterattack, in two other accounts, Chamberlain mentioned that an enemy force left the entrenchments to make an attempt on his left flank. Artillery commander, Wainwright confirms this unsuccessful enemy offensive.

I lay now straight out on my back, too weak to move a limb; the blood forming a pool, under and around me — more blood than the books allow a man. I had not much pain. It was more a stunning blow, a kind of dull tension, my teeth shut sharp together hard, like lock-jaw. So I lay looking, thinking, sinking, the tornado tearing over and around. Dull hoarse faint cries in the low air: hisses, spatters, thuds, thunderbolts mingling earth and sky, and I moistening the little space of mother-earth for a cabbage-garden for some poor fellow, black or white, unthinking, unknowing. I had lain here an hour, perhaps, when I was aware of some men standing over me, with low-toned voices debating with themselves what to do. I spoke to them. They brightened up, and said they were sent to bring me off the field. I told them it was of no good; I was not worth it, emphasizing this in such terms that they replied that they had positive orders. I told them I would give orders for them to go back. "Begging pardon," they said "but you are not in command now." This rather roused me, which only seemed to prove to them that I was worth saving. I told them they could not get up that slope without getting killed, every one of them. But they took me up, put me on their stretcher, and started. [We were] not 20 yards away when came one of those great shots from the Fort on the left [Ft. Mahone] striking in the very spot from which they had lifted me, and digging a grave there large enough for all us, scattering the earth and gravel all over us, with rather unpleasant force. The next minute a musket ball broke an arm for one of my carriers. Another took his place, and they steered for the right of the batteries, around which they managed to pass and set me down behind the batteries, below the range of shot skimming overhead. Captain Bigelow gave me all the attention possible, which was more relief to him than practical avail to me, a limp mass of bloody earth.[24]

---

24. One may assume that while profuse bleeding threatened Chamberlain's life, he had also lost enough blood to cause a drop in blood pressure, which would eventually slow his loss of blood. It apparently amused Chamberlain to ponder over what humble crop had eventually been nourished by his lifeblood at Petersburg, for after revisiting the same scene many years later, he wrote, "...I came upon a little bunch of sassafras bushes, rather lavishly nourished, it seemed, and I cut one of them to serve, like pansies — 'for thoughts.'" Regarding his artillerymen's actions, Bigelow would write to Chamberlain many years after the war, "The distinguished services, which you have rendered since the war, both to your state and to the College, which is honored by being under your charge, are abundant evidences that it is better to follow, on a battle field, the order of a well Captain than those of a wounded General." While Fort Sedgwick became known as Fort Hell, the Rebel Fort Mahone, #29, was christened Fort Damnation. Chamberlain offered that the "matter-of-fact men of both sides" chose the names of these two forts that "became famous all through the siege as the hottest point of contact of the hostile lines."

After a while an ambulance came galloping up to the foot of the hill, and I was put into it, and galloped through rough stumpy fields to a cluster of pines where our Division had a rude field hospital. Most of the surgeons there had been or were attached to my headquarters, and I knew and loved them, for they were noble men. The first thing done was to lay me upon a table improvised from a barn-window or door, and examine the wound. I remember somebody taking a ram rod of a musket and running it through my body — it [the wound] was too wide for any surgeon's probe — to discover the bullet, which they did not at first observe sticking up with a puff of skin just behind my left hip joint. This they soon cut out, and closed the cut with a bandage. Some slight dressing was put upon the round hole on the right side, and I was gently laid on a pile of pine boughs. Several badly wounded officers both of our army and of the Confederate were [around me]. On my right, his feet touching mine, noble Colonel Prescott of the 32 Massachusetts, with a bullet in his breast; on the other side, a fine-faced, young Confederate officer, badly wounded and suffering terribly. The whole little space was strewn thick with such cases as these. As the shadows grew thick, a group of surgeons stood not far off earnestly discussing something, looking at me now and then. I knew what it was. One of them said to another; "You do it." "No. I can't" was the reply. But I beckoned one of them to me and said, "I know all about it. You have done your best. It is a mortal wound. I know this, and am prepared for it. I have been for a long time." "Yes, there is no possible chance for you. We could not tell you. You can not live till morning." "So be it, you can't help me. But you can save poor Prescott; look to him. We won't leave you, Prescott," I turned to say — with voice rather feeble for such stout proffer of aid. "And here is this poor fellow, this rebel officer, suffering much. Help him all you can. He is far from home. He is ours now."[25]

I had got a leaf from a field order book and written with a pencil a brief letter to my young wife; telling her how it was; bidding her and our two little ones to God's keeping, and folded my hands with nothing more for them to do.[26]

It was a lurid, wild, cloud-driven sunset — like my own. Griffin came over to me with Bartlett and I think Warren and some of the Corps staff. Griffin did not know what to say. Indeed there was nothing to say, of the future, or of the present — and what avail now, of the past? I think I spoke first, and it may seem strange in such circumstances that I should begin almost playfully; "Well, General, you see I was right. Here I am, at the end. And here you are, as I knew you would be. But it is time to report. I have carried the crest."

25. There were not enough ambulances to take all the wounded at Petersburg to City Point, and while rank had its privileges, Chamberlain may well have been considered too seriously injured to make the trip. When Chamberlain was carried into the hospital tent of Dr. Robert Everett of the 16th Michigan [3rd Brigade, 1st Division, 5th Corps], the doctors began to have Corp. James Stettler of the 143rd Pennsylvania removed from the surgeon's table. Stettler had been severely wounded by the same shell that had struck Chamberlain's horse that morning during the 1st Brigade's first attack, and he would eventually lose his right foot three inches above the ankle. Stettler would recall Chamberlain's protest, "Lay me [to] one side; I am all right. Go and take care of my dear boys," but Stettler was removed, and the doctors placed Chamberlain upon the table. While Dr. Everett claimed to be the first surgeon to attend him, Dr. William R. DeWitt of Pennsylvania prepared the report of his treatment at the 1st Division Hospital. While it is apparent that Dr. DeWitt was a 1st Division surgeon, and it is likely that he had served with a Pennsylvania regiment, that regiment remains unidentified. Chamberlain, having commanded both, would have been familiar with the surgeons of both the 1st and 3rd Brigades. "Prescott" was George Lincoln Prescott, colonel of the 32nd Massachusetts, Sweitzer's 2nd Brigade, 1st Division, 5th Corps, who was wounded leading his regiment during the 2nd Brigade's charge that morning. Prescott died the next day, and a fort bearing his name was built on the ground the 32nd had gained on June 18. Spear of the 20th Maine would later recall of his visit to the hospital that night that Prescott, who sat opposite Chamberlain, was propped up writing a letter of farewell to his family. Chamberlain, whose chance of survival apparently seemed far less likely than Prescott's, would write of him in his book Passing of the Armies, "...Prescott, of the 32nd Massachusetts, who lay touching feet with me after mortal Petersburg of June 18th, under the midnight requiem of the somber pines — I doomed of all to go, and bidding him stay — but the weird winds were calling otherwise..." From the very first weeks of his service, Chamberlain had apparently given thought to his chances of losing his life on the battlefield. After experiencing the sights of combat for the first time at Antietam in 1862, Chamberlain wrote to his wife, Fanny, "...tomorrow we expect to be in the thickest of it all day & as for me I do not at all expect to escape injury. I hope I should not fall: but if it should be God's will I believe I can say amen. I think of you all whom I love so much & I know how you would wish me to bear myself in the field. I go, as twice today I went serious and anxious but not afraid. God be with you & with me." Back at the front on the night of June 18, the men of the 5th Corps spent the night gathering in their dead and wounded. The survivors of the Federal attacks on the Rebel fortifications made their way back to safety, under the cover of the night and smoke of the artillery that fired long into the night. To straighten their lines as Meade had ordered, many would withdraw from the ground they had taken during the day to the positions from which they had attacked that morning. Since so many officers were casualties, a lack of reports made it difficult to tabulate the losses of the AoP, but estimates for June 15-18 exceed 10,000. Casualty returns for Chamberlain's Brigade reported 314 killed, wounded, and missing, with the 187th Pennsylvania reporting a loss of 189 officers and men.

26. Chamberlain wrote to his wife, Fanny:

> My Darling wife I am lying mortally wounded the doctors think, but my mind & heart are at peace Jesus Christ is my all-sufficient savior. I go to him. God bless & keep & comfort you, precious one, you have been a precious wife to me. To know & love you makes life & death beautiful. Cherish the darlings & give my love to all the dear ones Do not grieve too much for me. We shall all soon meet Live for the children Give my dearest love to Father & mother Sallie & John Oh how happy to feel yourself forgiven God bless you ever-more precious precious one
>
> Ever yours Lawrence

In 1855, Joshua Chamberlain had married Frances Caroline Adams. The adopted daughter of a Brunswick, Maine, clergyman, Fanny, as she was called by her family and friends, was the daughter of Ashur and Amelia Adams of Jamaica Plains, Massachusetts. She was born on August 12, 1825. The "darlings" are Chamberlain's daughter, Grace Dupee [Daisy], born October 16, 1856, and son, Harold Wyllys, born October 11, 1858. Chamberlain's parents were Joshua Chamberlain, Jr. and Sarah Dupee Brastow Chamberlain of Brewer, Maine. "Sallie" is his sister, Sarah Brastow Chamberlain, born November 2, 1836. "John" is one of his brothers, John Calhoun Chamberlain, born August 1, 1838.

"You are going to pull through" he says. In spite of them all, you will pull through. It will come out all right," he says.

"Yes, but I would have had some things otherwise," I answered.

"Do you know," he eagerly returns, "Grant has promoted you! He has sent his word! He will write an order about it."

"Has he? That will not help me now. But it will do good. I thank the General. I thank you, and all of you for this kindness."

They spoke of my promotion and the manner of it. They did not know how narrowly I had escaped cashiering, as I did. They all spoke gentle words, some praisingly.

But Griffin came up near, took my hand and said: "Now keep a stiff upper lip. We will stand by you. Meade knows about it. It will be all right."

"Yes, General." — "Good Night." — "Good Night."

But I saw in the glimmering twilight his hand drawn across his eyes and his shoulder shiver and heave quite visibly, even to my fading eyes. Then I folded my hands again across my chest.[27]

---

27. A chaplain described a tearful Bartlett leaning over Chamberlain, and observed during Bartlett and Griffin's visit with Chamberlain and Prescott at the hospital that, "Officers who fear neither Mini balls or shell are nervous and childlike as they come back here." Bartlett commanded the 3rd Brigade, 1st Division, 5th Corps, which had formerly been Chamberlain's brigade. [See "The Charge at Fort Hell" annotation #2 for details.] Warren notified Meade of Chamberlain's wounding in a report sent in the evening of June 18. Chamberlain's description of his informing Griffin that he had taken the crest that he advanced upon the morning of June 18, provides yet another piece of contradictory evidence regarding DeLacy's claim that the order to attack at Rives' Salient came from Griffin. On June 19, Warren sent to Meade by telegraph: "Col. J. L. Chamberlain of the 20th Maine Regt, commanding the 1st Brigade of the 1st Division was mortally wounded, it is thought, in the assaults on the enemy yesterday, the ball having passed through the pelvis and bladder. He has been recommended for promotion for gallant and efficient conduct on previous occasions, and yesterday led his brigade against the enemy under most destructive fire. He expresses the wish that he may receive the recognition of his service by promotion before he died for the gratification his family and friends, and I beg that if possible it may be done. He has been sent to City Point. G. K. Warren, Maj Gen." [For earlier recommendations for Chamberlain's promotion, see Smith's *Fanny and Joshua*, pp. 367-68, en#6.] Meade forwarded Warren's request to Grant, with the following endorsement: "The above statement is transmitted to the lieutenant-general commanding with the earnest recommendation that Colonel Chamberlain's wish be gratified."

   Grant forwarded to Secretary of War Edwin Stanton, Warren's telegram and a copy of his special order promoting Chamberlain and asking for President Lincoln's sanction and that it be sent to the Senate for confirmation. Special Order #39 stated: "Col. Joshua L. Chamberlain, Twentieth Regiment Maine Infantry Volunteers, is, for meritorious and efficient services on the field of battle, and especially for gallant conduct in leading his brigade against the enemy at Petersburg, Va., on the 18th instant, in which he was dangerously wounded, hereby, in pursuance of authority from the Secretary of War, appointed a full brigadier-general of U.S. Volunteers, to rank as such from the 18th day of June, 1864, subject to the approval of the President of the United States." Chamberlain received a copy of this telegram from Grant upon his arrival at the naval hospital at Annapolis, Maryland. Many years later, a newspaper article would report that Chamberlain had at some point been told by Grant himself that this was the first battlefield promotion he had made, but of course, that honor was held by Col. Emory Upton of the 6th Corps. Grant appointed Upton a brigadier general of volunteers weeks earlier at Spotsylvania.

After a while of this stupor suddenly came a flood of tearing agony. I never dreamed what pain could be and not kill a man outright. My pity went back to men I had seen helpless on the stricken field. The pain wore into a stupor. Then through the mists I looked up and saw dear, faithful Doctor Shaw, Surgeon of my own regiment [the 20th Maine] lying a mile away. My brother Tom had brought him. He and good Dr. Townsend sat down by me and tried to use some instrument to establish proper connection to stop the terrible extravasations which would end my life. All others had given it up, and me too. But these two faithful men bent over their task trying with vain effort to find the entrance to torn and clogged and distorted passages of vital currents. Toiling and returning to the ever impossible task, the able surgeon undertaking to aid Dr. Shaw said, sadly, "It is of no use, Doctor; he cannot be saved. I have done all possible for man. Let us go, and not torture him longer." "Just once more, Doctor; let me try just this once more, and I will give it up." Bending to his task, by a sudden miracle, he touched the exact lost thread; the thing was done. There was a possibility, only that even now, that I might be there to know in the morning. Tom stood over me like a brother, and such a one as he was. True-hearted Spear with him, watching there like guardians over a cradle amidst the wolves of the wilderness.[28]

After midnight I became aware of some one fumbling about my beard, trying to find my mouth. The great iron spoon made its way along the uncertain track made by his trembling hand. I opened my eyes and there knelt Spear, his red beard in the gleam of a lurid camp-fire making him look like a picture of one of the old masters. He had been turning the spoon bowl as he thought in the right place, but had missed it by an inch, and the beverage he was offering had taken the course nearest to the earth, which was down my neck and bosom out-side. "Now. please give me some," I plaintively murmured, taking a little cheer, if I can be believed, in making a joke of it. The tears were running down his cheeks, and I thought, into the black tin dipper; but he smiled through them — and taken all together, it was a good por-ridge. At times the agonizing pains would get the better of my patience. But sufferings of those lying around me, particularly of the poor for-lorn southerner close to me, were some counterpoise. "A fellow-feel-ing makes us wondrous kind." At dawn dear brave Prescott was dead, and I alive. Griffin had been stirring. Meade had sent a stretcher and 8 men to carry me 16 miles to City Point, to be taken by steamer to

28. Dr. Abner O. Shaw of Maine, after serving as a private in the 7th New York Regiment, was an 1863 graduate of the College of Physicians and Surgeons in New York City. He began serving as an assistant surgeon with the 20th Maine shortly after Gettysburg, soon to be promoted to surgeon. Tom was Chamberlain's youngest brother, Thomas Davee Chamberlain, born April 29, 1841. Tom enlisted as a private in the 20th Maine at the organization of the regiment but was soon promoted to sergeant. In early 1863, he was appointed 1st lieutenant of Co. "G" and served as his brother, Col. Chamberlain's, acting adjutant at Gettysburg. For his efficiency and gallantry at that battle, Tom Chamberlain was promoted to captain of Co. "G," the office he held throughout the campaign of 1864. He later served as provost marshal of the 1st Division, 5th Corps, and in 1865 was commissioned lieutenant colonel of the 20th Maine. Dr. Morris Townsend of New York, was an 1853 graduate of Jefferson Medical College of Philadelphia. He served as surgeon of the 47th New York before becoming surgeon of the 44th New York, which served with the 20th Maine in the 3rd Brigade, 1st Division, 5th Corps. While the historian of the 44th New York credits Dr. Townsend with saving Chamberlain's life at Petersburg, it was widely believed, particularly by the patient himself, that Dr. Shaw provided the final vital treatment. Chamberlain's remarkable choice of words may call for translation. "Extravasations," in this case refers to bleeding, while the "torn and clogged and distorted passages of vital currents" are damaged blood vessels. "True-hearted Spear" is Ellis Spear of Bowdoin Medical School's class of 1858, who entered service in the 20th Maine as captain of Co. "G," the company he himself had raised for the regiment. Promoted to major in August of 1863, Spear often had command of the 20th Maine, but the tenacity with which the frequently absent Lt. Col. Charles Gilmore clung to the 20th Maine prevented further promotion for Spear. Finally receiving a brevet appointment of lieutenant colonel for meritorious services, Spear left the 20th Maine briefly, on recruiting duty in Maine. He then returned to the front to take command of 198th Pennsylvania in Chamberlain's 1st Brigade, the command Spear held at Appomattox Court House in April of 1865. When Chamberlain was given command of the ANV's formal surrender, ironically it was his old 3rd Brigade, including the 20th Maine, to which Chamberlain gave a place of honor during the surrender. Spear did not return to the 20th Maine and the 3rd Brigade until Gilmore finally resigned in May of 1865. At that point, Spear, who had been appointed a brevet colonel for gallant conduct at Quaker Road, could finally be mustered in as the 20th Maine's colonel. In 1899, when he wrote "The Charge at Fort Hell," Chamberlain obviously still held the feelings of friendship and comradeship for Spear that they had maintained for many years. Sadly, in the coming years, Spear would come to publicly belittle and contradict Chamberlain's accounts of the war, to the point where Spear even began to contradict his own contemporary accounts. After his old commander's death in 1914, the tone of Spear's correspondence takes on the tone of a personal vendetta.

Bangor Public Library

Maj. Tom Chamberlain

Annapolis. That was thought the only way to save me. If I could be got into a tent by the seashore, with skillful treatment, and favorable surroundings, there might be a chance for me. Friends gathered to see my "forlorn hope" move out. It was a blazing day. My bearers were none too many. I felt Meade's kind thoughtfulness. This was probably Griffin's doing, although the order for the detail came from Meade. The great loss of blood had weakened me to the extreme. The men tried to screen my face from the burning sun, and to relieve my faintness by moistened cl[oths] laid over it. But it was a hard day for them — this 16 miles march with this wearying load. I wish I could have had the names of those men so as to follow them in life.[29]

At City Point I was transferred to a steamer — my stretcher set down on the main deck. I was told there were 600 badly wounded officers on board. There was something in the air which testified this, both to the senses and to the mysterious "inner sense." I felt the whole, as well as my part, of the mournful embassy. The thought, too, of the

---

29. In his recollections written after the turn of the century, Spear would relate that it was a chaplain, rather than himself, who had administered soup to Chamberlain that night. See annotation #25 for identification of "Prescott." Dr. Townsend of the 44th New York accompanied Chamberlain to City Point. In paragraph #27 of "The Charge at Fort Hell," Chamberlain offers additional evidence that Griffin was in large part responsible for his transportation to City Point, and thus to Annapolis Hospital. Located at the convergence of the James and Appomattox Rivers, City Point was a village of fewer than one hundred residents before the war, which served as Petersburg's river port, until it was occupied by Butler's AoJ in early May of 1864. Several days after the Battle of Petersburg, Grant officially designated City Point as the main supply base for all military operations against Petersburg. It was likely at City Point that Chamberlain first saw the New York newspapers which had printed long notices and an editorial describing how he had died. Chamberlain would remember, "It was quite cheerful reading for a live man I can assure you." The hospital he was sent to was at the Naval Academy in Annapolis, Maryland.

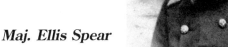

Maj. Ellis Spear

Maine State Archives

"government" taking care of us stricken, broken bodies, was grateful.
But the journey was long, and the night and morning dreary. The surgeon in charge had braced himself for his task a little too much, and
came near going over backwards. We — the people on my deck —
suffered for lack of proper care. We were in wretched condition —
broken, maimed, torn, stiffened with clotted blood and matted hair and
beard, dazed with that strange sensation of being suddenly cut down
from the full flush of vigorous health to hardly breathing bodies.

We did not know what we wanted — nor did anybody else, apparently. But by some fortunate accident Dr. Tom Moses, one of my old
College boys who had charge of the upper deck, learned that I was
below, and he lost no time in coming to my side; and he was virtually
there all that dismal night.[30]

---

30. Chamberlain was put aboard the Steamer *Connecticut*. Maj. George Merrick of the 187th
    Pennsylvania, who would lose a leg from his wounding on June 18, occupied a cot next to
    his commander's. He remembered Chamberlain's words to him about the 187th. "Major,
    I want to commend the Regiment that you commanded; I want to commend that Regi-
    ment that became veterans in a day. No Regiment with whatever experience could have
    performed their duty more nobly than they did. You were simply willing to take orders
    and hold your ground under tremendous odds, and that was the best proof of heroism."
    The surgeon in charge of the *Connecticut* has not been identified, but Thomas Freeman
    Moses was a member of Bowdoin Medical School's class of 1857, a classmate of
    Chamberlain's brother, Horace. Moses graduated from Jefferson Medical College in Phila-
    delphia in 1861, and served in the army as an acting assistant surgeon from 1862 to 1864.
    After the war, he was a professor at Urbana University in Ohio, and its president in the
    last years of the century.

LOC

Steamer Connecticut

Bowdoin College Special Collection

Dr. Tom Moses

It seemed to me some time after the second midnight that I was set on the wharf at Annapolis Naval School, and left there a long time before my turn came, and then it was to be taken into a naked dreary tent. There I lay entirely alone for hours. The first disturbance I had was seeing the flap of my tent open and a kindly, earnest face looking in, and then the whole form of woman's divineness came to me, with the question, "Who are you?" If she had said "What are you," it would have been justified. A more uncanny looking being, I suppose, never stood across a human pathway. "Booted and spurred," blood-soaked and smeared, hair and beard matted with blood and earth, where I had lain on the earth amidst the flying turf and stones, pale as death and weak as water — I was a poor witness of what I was, or who. But from that moment no tenderness that man or angel could show was left unfulfilled by this Boston girl, Mary Clark. She interested Dr. Vanderkieft in my case, & he sent Welsh "Tommy" to serve me, and I had all the surgical skill that the French army or the United States could command, and all the care that divine womanhood could divine. But it was a "far cry to Lochow." For two months wrestling at the gates of death, in agonies inexpressible, though direfully enough betokened, convulsions, death-chills, lashings, despairing surgeons, waiting embalmers — "rejected addresses" — and all this under the eyes of the dear, suffering wife, who had taken up her dwelling in the adjoining tent. Through this valley of the shadow of death — in five months back at the front with my men![31]

---

31. Chamberlain arrived at the Naval School Hospital in Annapolis on June 20. Mary T. Clark of Jamaica Plain, which was a satellite of Boston but is now part of the city proper, would remain a lifelong friend of the Chamberlains. The pain he suffered while under her care caused Mary to express "wonder why God allowed it." [For more information on Chamberlain/Clark relationships, see *Fanny and Joshua*.] Dr. Bernard Albert Vanderkieft, a native of Holland, came to the United States around the beginning of the Civil War. Though nothing is known of his history before coming to America, it is likely that Chamberlain is referring to Dr. Vanderkieft when he speaks of "all the surgical skill that the French army or the United States could command." After coming to America, Vanderkieft served with the 53rd and the 102nd New York Regiments before having charge of military hospitals in Annapolis, and later in Baltimore. In 1865, Chamberlain would write a letter of recommendation for Vanderkieft's promotion to lieutenant colonel. Nothing came to light to identify Chamberlain's attendant, "Welsh 'Tommy'." All that could be discovered of the expression a "far cry to Lochow," is that it may be a variation on "a far cry to Lochore," a phrase apparently still heard in the British military. One is tempted to consider that the change from "Lochore" to "Lochow" may have phonetic roots in Maine locals' propensity for dropping the final "R" from their words. Lochore is a village across the Firth of Forth from Edinburgh, an area known for its outstanding beauty. The phrase is a tongue-in-cheek comment on any place or situation that is a long way from being pleasant or comfortable. The bullet that struck Chamberlain damaged his urethra. It was so near the juncture of the penis and scrotum that it might have opened the wound that, due to prolonged use of a catheter, developed into a fistula, an abnormal tract or opening. In this case, it lead from the damaged urethra out to the surface of the skin. Chamberlain not only experienced leakage of urine from the fistula, but also through the original track of the bullet, urine coursing out through the entrance wound on his right hip. During his hospital stay, he endured severe infection of the wound and urosepsis, an infection in the urinary system, both of which would have caused chills and high fever. In those days before antiseptic treatment and antibiotics, it is impressive that he survived. Fanny Chamberlain, pregnant with their fifth child, reached Annapolis with two of her friends soon after Chamberlain's arrival and stayed with him until his release from the hospital on September 20. Chamberlain, after recuperating at his home, left Brunswick to return to the field on October 29, four months and eleven days after he was wounded at Petersburg.

James Frasca collection

Frances Caroline Adams Chamberlain

NARA

Brig. Gen. Joshua L. Chamberlain

APPENDIX A

EXERT FROM "REMINISCENCES OF PETERSBURG AND APPOMATTOX: OCTO-
BER, 1903" BY BREVET MAJOR-GENERAL JOSHUA L. CHAMBERLAIN [WAR
PAPERS (PORTLAND: LEFAVOR-TOWER CO., 1908), III.]

I am honored that you think it of interest to hear the recital of some
impressions made upon me by a recent visit to Petersburg and
Appomattox Court House, Virginia, the first and the last battle-fields of
the final campaign of the Army of the Potomac and the Army of Northern Virginia.

I have no reason to expect that what most drew my interest there will
equally command, or deserve, yours. My motive was primarily personal;
to assure myself as to two certain points on those fields, the last visions of
which had left my memory somewhat clouded — the one, with the sudden overcast of my own early down-going amidst storm and disaster; the
other, with the thrilling phantasmagoria of the consummation. I am not
trying to write history; nor, indeed, to write at all. I am yielding to the
mood of the hour; letting these scenes review me as much as I them —
what is unchanged testing the changed. Pardon me if the personal element in this recital may seem a blemish upon the description.

I wished especially to revisit the ground of the first few days' fighting before Petersburg, in June, 1864. This embraced scarcely more
than a tenth part of what afterwards became our entrenched line. But
we do not quite realize what storied and bloody ground that first three
days' fighting made. The Union losses within those days were a hundred and twenty-eight in a thousand. Compare this with other fields
more famous; with our losses at Spotsylvania, for example, which in
the whole struggle were in the ration of a hundred and eight to a thousand; or with that at the slaughter-pen of Cold Harbor, which was a
hundred and eleven in a thousand. This higher rate of a hundred and
twenty-eight in a thousand shows sharp work for our first dash at Petersburg, and the casualty list of ten thousand men of those engaged in
that overture gives this some rank among battles and battle-fields, without counting what followed in the long siege and sojourn there.

NARA

Union soldiers standing on earthworks of Fort Sedgwick (Fort Hell) after the fall of Petersburg, April, 1865.

It may seem strange that on my return from a somewhat protracted removal, I should not have taken early occasion, to visit this region in cool blood — if there was any of that left — in order to find justification of my former opinion as to the nature of that position, and that attack. The explanation is two-fold: first that immediately on my return I was sent to the extreme left of our ever leftward creeping line, and in that way was so closely occupied until the end of it all, that I could not get a day off for seeing old curiosities; and the other reason, quite as effective — that during the whole feverish siege thereafter, the conditions were not encouraging; no man could show his head above the parapets or outside the bomb-proofs and keep it level a moment, unless with, and of the dead —

the two limits of my early operations having been appropriately named by those later domiciled there, Fort Hell and Fort Damnation, two places, or conditions, I desired to form the habit of avoiding.

The relations which your kindness has established for this occasion makes me desirous of bringing them still nearer, that our minds may take up this review from the same point of vision. In other words, I desire to recall to your minds the reason and manner in which we came to be here at all.

The movement on Petersburg, as you know, was intended to be a surprise, and a success. The old plan of operations — across the Virginia rivers, Richmond the objective, with the perpetual side-issue of "not uncovering Washington," which made our successive steps of advance a zig-zag, like the knight's move on the chess-board, and our whole grand tactics a horizontal ricochet along the enemy's front from left to right, a series of operations of which Grant had said he would "fight it out on this line, if it took all summer" — had been pretty thoroughly executed. A most memorable summer it made for us; and a casualty list of seventy thousand men indicated that it had been "fought out" pretty well by our army. Certainly some climax had been reached in Grant's mind; for he suddenly and courageously changed his plan altogether; swinging his army across the James River, for a bold dash to flank Richmond by way of Petersburg, cutting Lee's communications and forcing him from his base instead of consolidating him upon it. This was a masterly move, and ought to have been successful. Strikingly it was so at the first. The advance of our army got fairly in front of Petersburg before Lee knew we were across the James. Beauregard was then holding the defenses of Petersburg, with only Wise's Legion, of twenty-four hundred men, and Dearing's cavalry and some picked-up men, about as many more. We could have walked right into the city at the first dash; and would have done it, as the desperate valor and direful cost two days afterwards proved.

But Grant expected Butler to do this, from his advantageous position on the James, nearby. Indeed, the Eighteenth Corps under "Baldy" Smith did make a successful attack from this direction, carrying the enemy's works on the northeast side of the city, but strangely stopped. Meade had not been told that his army was to take a direct part with Butler, but ordered Hancock, with our Second Corps, as soon as he got rations after crossing, to proceed to a designated spot, which proved to be incorrectly laid down on the maps, and if it had any existence at all was miles away from his proper direction and inside the enemy's lines. In this situation

Hancock was overtaken by an order from Grant to go to the assistance of Smith, but arrived only after dark, when it was Smith's opinion too late to follow up his advantage. Had Meade been informed of what might be expected, Hancock and the Second Corps would have been inside of Petersburg when the sunset gilded its spires, and the fate of that field and of many a man in our army would have been far different from what followed. This matter never has been understood. Grant, we knew, was much vexed at the turn of things this day; but was wonderfully patient, as if blaming nobody but himself.

Thus the golden moment was lost. Our several corps, meanwhile crossing the James by pontoons and transports, marching day and night, coming up successively into position as "on right into line," attacked as soon as each found the enemy's front. This was not difficult to find, for Lee was now rapidly reinforcing Beauregard, so that each corps as it came up had to meet at least an equal number of Lee's old army, on interior lines, well covered by strong entrenchments. The Second and Ninth Corps worked in their own stalwart fashion, forcing the enemy's advanced positions. Our Fifth Corps came up on the next night, and passing in the rear of these, attacked on the left; but by that time all Lee's army were before us. So we had to take up the old game — the eternal feeling to the left, with continuous, costly, fruitless engagements, in wearisome monotony. The conditions of the situation compelling us to throw up breastworks, our entrenched line came to extend more than sixteen miles, and we were forced to "sit down" as it is whimsically called, and this case most literally, and in rather hard-bottomed chairs — to an irregular siege of more than nine months. And in all that time we got no nearer to Petersburg than we were on the eighteenth of June, 1864, and not until Lee was flanked at Five Forks, April 1, 1865.

Quite different this from a "surprise." And with experiences not yet written in history, though grimly registered by nature herself in a thousand fantastic forms far outstrewn, making the dreary stretch seem like a haunted land. And truly indeed may it be so; when we remember that twenty-two thousand brave spirits of ours left their bodies there behind those treeclumps and on the slopes before those rueful works of man.

Now thirty-nine years was time enough to cool one's blood, so as to gather the various data for mature judgment more reliable perhaps than confused recollections of personal experience. Reminding myself, too, that things, also as well as men, may change somewhat in that lapse of years, I deemed it expedient to take a guide, and one a little more calm and collected than those of previous occasions there, when the staff officers bringing orders scarcely dared to lift their chins from their breastbones. So I got an intelligent citizen of Petersburg who had made a special study of this ground and its history, to take me in his much-enduring, gig-like vehicle along the strangely half-hidden lines, whose wonted tumult seemed to me only half-hushed, waiting the moment to burst into roar and flame.

We first drove out over the old Confederate ground to the vicinity of the "Hare house," the scene of repeated desperate struggle, begun and continued by our Second Corps. The thing that most took my attention was a shapely white monument shining in the midst of a grove of young oaks sombered with the tints of autumn. Seeking a nearer view, I was deeply moved to find it the monument of the 1st Maine Heavy Artillery, serving here then as infantry, and serving ever since, I may say, as high example of heroic valor. It marks the scene of a gallant fight — or in more exact statement, of superb courage and sublime obedience in making a charge against overwhelming odds under an order which should not have been given. The regimental association, I was told, had bought five acres of this storied ground, and set up this monument to the immortal honor of more than six hundred of its men who fell in that one onset, and were buried in the earth beneath, uptorn by plunging shot and shell. This memorial is the more impressive for being the only monument erected as such — with thoughtful purpose, and honoring remembrance, on the entire field. The sight of it was a fitting overture for the tragic reminiscences of the day before me. This, indeed, was the surprise — that so broad a field of heroic devotion and costly sacrifice should call for no monuments to perpetuate remembrance or consecrate ground. It seems to fall out of view, like "patient continuance in well-doing."

The first broad aspect of this ground is not impressive; there is so much of it, and of such sameness or repetition. Large stretches of rolling surface; gently confronting slopes descending to some branch or run draining the rain-wash and underground springs towards the tributaries of the Appomattox. Only rarely a house or hunt, and scarcely a cultivated field, in the entire extent. But the most striking feature is that the whole ground looks strangely cut up with hedge-like lines of shrubbery running in queer directions not suggested by the natural lay of the land, nor its present uses; with rows of rugged oaks and scattered tufts of evergreens; wild, uncut grasses grave-yard like, in patches here and there; all giving to the face of things a wrinkled and haggard look.

But coming nearer one sees that these hedges mark the sites of old picket lines, rifle pits and breastworks; shallow trench and low parapet grown over not only with native herbage, but with apple, pear, peach and plum, sprung from seeds sown in the long days and nights when such luxuries found their way to the men on the sharp-edged front, with not much room between their faces and the bare earth; and that these heavy clumps of trees, mostly evergreens, many as large as cannon or nail-kegs, have sprung up by some hidden law of nature from the deeper loosened earth around the batteries, bomb-proofs, mortar-pits, and covered ways, wherein men used to be put to their wit's end how not to be knocked out of their five senses. As those old scenes rise before us, the contrast makes the picture more dramatic.

For here when last seen by me before, on the one side and the other, mighty masses and serried ranks of brave, true men stood, and struck, and went willingly to death for what they, strangely contrariwise, deemed the right; conflict of the deep-felt and the far-seen in principles, interests and ideals, out of which the new nation was to emerge. It was the travail of the people. This is no too strong a figure. For was not this undergone? Sorrow, suffering, sacrifice, surrender, devotion, death — that something for the world's good should be born into being? Know you not that the tears of this were drawn up into the heavens to descend on these fields in the ever new-creating rains to consecrate this mingled blood to the building of "the house not made with hands," here upon the earth? But for such thought, how desolating would this vision be!

And of the thousands left buried there, not all forgotten! I saw all along the edge of the trenches, in the fringe of the grasses and thickets, little hillocks, sunken oblongs of earth, familiar, unmistakable to experienced eyes. Now and then, strange to see, a drooping flower placed lately at the head by far-remembering love, or a wild rose planted by some unknowing but caring heart, or nature's own sweet hand.

Passing amidst these relics and mementos, where nature buries what she wishes to preserve, we wonder what it is that is most abiding. Here after Vesuvian convulsions, men are gone; things remain. The mighty actors are suddenly lifted from the scene and their works stand, silent, rugged, realistic, unadorned; truthful monitors of tremendous struggle. I should not say unadorned, for nature has touched them with her own adornment; hillocks which were walls of thundering, havoc-dealing cannon, now thickly overgrown with peaceful pines sighing in the soft winds; the shallow trenches far-stretching or queerly curved and angled, once breasted with brave hearts and fringed with fire, now fringed by soft embroidery of growing plants, with varied threads, rich in texture, form and color; the slopes and middle grounds which ran red with blood, now veiled with grasses strangely rank and vital; nature's subtle alchemy and ever-brooding spirit transmuting into new, calm life, the bodies of the thousands once battling for peace under law — of which this multiform peace of nature is the ghost or adumbration.

There is a peculiar impressiveness about the forsaken. Some deep places in us are more moved by a forlorn field like this than by a glorified one like Gettysburg. At any rate, the contrast is wide and striking. There, action concentrated, intense, decisive; here, struggle long-drawn, persistent, indecisive; there, the mighty stake, the destinies of nations determined by the issue of an hour; here, stubborn patience, tireless fortitude, unflinching gaze at overwhelming death days and nights and months together, to test the merits of a tactical plan. Then as to material, visible elements; at Gettysburg, the constructive work of man uppermost; at Petersburg, the covering work of nature. That, made a magnificent mausoleum, a splendid spectacle; this, the bald fact, held fast, as cased in amber; there highest art in headstone, monument and statue; here, grim trees, wild grasses, clinging mosses; there, luxurious avenues laid out for artistic effect, or convenience of visitors, even though confusing the old battle-lines; here only the very lines themselves, laid out by daring courage or desperate need, and behind them the footworn paths carpeted now by fallen leaf and ripened cone; there, the remaining gathered in a noble cemetery consecrated with immortal eloquence, cherished in eternal honor; here, sleeping in their blood, canopied by swaying branches growing out of it, the last resting-place marked by the chance staying of some wild rose, named only by the birds singing love-notes above them. There, all remembered; here, all but forgotten! Which is grandest, most magnificent, I am not asking. Which is most impressive, I claim not to decide. That depends on the man, or the mood. I have memories of both, but hold largely of the forgotten.

Except the trees and shrubbery that had grown up on the battle-lines, the face of things on our side seemed but little changed. In very few places field had replaced forest, or forest field. In some favored spots, then fallow, new fields had been laid out, chiefly where the ground had been furrowed and fertilized by the harrowings of nine months' siege and sortie. Going over some of these, the earth having been loosened or beaten down by recent heavy rains, I saw now and then a bullet or fragment of shell washed to the surface. This, even, now — although for years the neighboring residents had made it a business to gather such relics, at first in quantities to pay for carting away and selling for profit as metal. And still, in the few poor little homes set up here and there along the lines by the cultivators of the grounds, the revenue from these now gathered sold as relics, helps materially in making up the margin of their little livelihood. I bought some of them, out of charity, or compliment, or compliance with evident expectation. The inhabitants of these houses are said to be Union men's families. But by what tenure or tolerance holding; whether relics of the war or products of later circumstances, I forbore to ascertain.

The principal crops on the old battle slopes are sweet potatoes, corn and peanuts — there's monumental glory for you! I was told these were all very profitable, especially the later, not requiring as yet replenishment of fertilizers since the old lavish top-dressing of human bodies and sharp cross-harrowing of cannon. Indeed, I saw many a bone that once helped make up a stalwart man, scattered, half-buried over these fields, yielding up its lime and phosphates for body and brain of people hardly the equals of those which these elements had braced for great things done and suffered. But this illustrates that strange law of exchange in human economics — the greater given for the less. In certain spots specially and significantly fertile, which could bear the tasking, tobacco is the best paying crop. And smoke of this being solace for sorrows and substance of daydreams has wide demands.

On the other side, as a general rule, the old Confederate fortifications, lying nearer town, are mostly obliterated. Here the ground lies for the most part better to the sun. It seems also to have a more substantial soil for cultivation. The proximity of the prosperous, growing city has naturally created a demand for these lands. Their soldier-dead are gathered in the conspicuous and beautiful cemetery. The battle mounds are mostly leveled, and the wounds healed. Farther out, where the two lines nearly met, are some stark relics still.

The hostile lines were, on the average, about a mile apart. But at certain important points they narrowed in to close range distance. In such places, after the daily experiences of being raked with shot and shell, pounded with mortars, and chopped up with canister and musketry, the men so close at hand could join in each others' psalm-singing, and perhaps more personal exhortations across the breastworks and rifle-pits until the grim guardians of the night took up their watch.

The batteries and mortars, of course, were not always placed with a view to immediate effect, but occasionally to collateral or remote effect, being so disposed as best to keep down the fire of some annoying battery of the opponent, or effectually to enfilade any advance or sortie from a position otherwise advantageous for such movement, or perhaps to protect their own infantry front by a sweeping cross-fire. Such a battery, or mortar-pit, might be a mile away from any obvious need in its immediate front. So the pieces on this checkered board were curiously set for a wide play of arms.

What I especially wished to see was the part of the Confederate line called Rives' Salient, and the ground opposite, which was the point of the extreme advance of our army on June 18, 1864. This position, on the outskirts of the city, covered the approaches of the Norfolk Railroad and the Jerusalem Plank Road, two of the enemy's most important lines of communication toward the sea, and, of course, was very strongly fortified.

As you are kindly offering to share some of the emotions with which I revisited this scene, I may be justified in not omitting what I had recalled and recorded here, as to some points in the action of the day referred to, which by reason of the troubled ending of that day have not been brought out in official reports, or popular war sketches; relating, indeed, mostly to personal history of no great moment outside a very narrow circle, which you now do me the honor of broadening.

When, on the evening of June 17, under the sharp attack of our Second and Ninth Corps, the enemy drew in the outer line of their defenses, they left on an outlying crest near the "Deep Cut" of the Norfolk Railroad, an advanced artillery post, commanding the approaches from our side, to the fortifications at Rives' Salient. From this position early on the eighteenth, they opened a strong slant fire on our division then drawn up for an assault in our immediate front north of the railroad. Our attack was thus delayed while our own batteries were getting into position to support this assault. Our line, however, was held in place — perhaps to take the enemy's attention from the movement of our guns. This raking fire along our ranks was very trying to the nerves, as well as to our judgment of the tactics which held us there, when we were not allowed to move forward nor to hit back — I am not saying, to get back! Our men were going down fast, and for no good, that we could see. It was therefore a welcome piece of information when our corps commander came along with the euphemistic statement that this was "very annoying;" which remark prefaced the suave inquiry if I thought I could carry that position.

I understood the purport of the mild inquiry. "Thought," indeed, was required; but the meaning was action. The enemy's fire had an unobstructed range over a clear slope of ground, and the deep cut between us forbade a straight-away rush. By a pardonable ruse of occupying their attention, we crossed the railroad south of the cut, gained a clump of woods on the flank of their guns, and by a sharp and hot, but short, encounter, we realized our commander's wish. We carried everything. But we found it a more perilous place to hold than to carry, for we were greeted by a storm of shot and shell from the enemy's main works at the Salient, under which we should soon lose more men than we did in carrying the position. I therefore drew the men back to gain the shelter of the crest, and disposed my lines front and flank for the best defense against expected counter assault.

Reconnoitering the situation I could see no likelihood of being able to hold this place long, nor in my judgment was it of importance to hold, now that batteries were dislodged which had annoyed our troops in the designed assault. Moreover, I discovered that the position was completely commanded by the enemy's main works at the Salient. Three or four hundred yards in our front were plainly seen several strong earthworks with twelve or fifteen guns so disposed as to deliver a smashing cross-fire over the ground between us, and just across the Plank Road was a large fort with heavy guns ready to sweep the crest we were occupying. Between these works was a solid entrenched infantry line of at least three thousand men. We were a mile away from the rest of the army, and I prepared to "take care of myself." I hurried up three batteries entrusted to me, running the guns up under cover of the crest, leveling slight platforms, on the hither slope, so that the men could work their guns, taking advantage of their recoil at discharge to reload, and easily run them up again, the muzzles lying in the grass — all as yet unperceived by the enemy — and made ready for what might happen. This position would be of use in case of a general assault by our army, and this was what I looked for.

At this juncture what was my astonishment at receiving a verbal order through a staff officer personally unknown to me, directing me in the name of "the general commanding" to assault the enemy's main works in my front with my brigade.

This was certainly a compliment to my six splendid regiments. But I think you will justify my astonishment, as well as my back-handed courage and recklessness of personal consequences in presuming to send back to the general a written statement of the situation with the opinion that that position could not be carried with a single brigade, even of Gettysburg veterans.

Grant had lost all patience that morning, and his chief subordinates were excited and flurried in a manner I had not seen before. I received, however, a courteous answer saying the whole army would join in on my right. But the single brigade was to make the assault, and prove the prophecy. In such an assault musketry was not to be thought of. It must be a storm of cannonade, a rush of infantry with pieces at the shoulder. Over the works and bayonet the enemy at their guns! It was desperate, deadly business. The bugler sounded the "charge." Under that storm of fire the earth flew into the air, men went down like scythe-swept grain; a wall of smoke veiled the front. I had thought it necessary to lead the charge, with full staff following; but in ten minutes not a man was left mounted. My staff were scattered; my flag-bearer shot dead, my own horse down. To cheer and guide the men, where no voice could be heard, nor rank distinguished, I picked up the flag and bore it aloft, till, close upon the enemy's works, a minie-ball cut me through, and the red cross came down to the reddened, riddled earth. I saw my men rush past me to the very muzzles of the guns, then torn in pieces and trickling back — the enemy rushing out beyond our left to flank our batteries on the crest behind us. I had only strength to send two broken regiments to support the batteries before I saw that all else was lost. In the midst of this seething turmoil I lay half-buried by clods of up-torn earth for an hour, when the shrouding smoke lifted, I was borne from the field by some of Major Bigelow's men of the Ninth Massachusetts Battery on the crest.

When you picture that field, air and earth cross-cut with thick-flying, hitting, plunging, burying, bursting missiles, you will not wonder that we did not succeed in "bayoneting the enemy at their guns inside their works." You will rather wonder that some of my men got near enough to fall within twenty feet of them.

I have given some detail to this description because this ground so taken and so fortified, was afterwards strongly entrenched, under that name "Fort Sedgwick," which together with the formidable work on my left front opposite, named Fort Mahone, became famous all through the siege as the hottest point of contact of the hostile lines. I have remarked to you that these places were rechristened with Bible names by the matter-of-fact men of both sides — not from poetic inspiration, nor romantic fancy, but in the old-fashioned style, from the most striking characteristic of the object, or its principal occupation.

It was interesting to go over this ground again after so many eventful years. The strength of this Fort Hell of ours was as much in the earth as in its guns, so it was well preserved. We found its walls pierced for twenty-five guns — fourteen four-and-one-half-inch Rodmans, thirty-pounders; two siege howitzers; eight field guns. This showed what was needed through the terrible siege; at long or short range — half musket shot distant from the entrenched infantry in front, and with a long reach on both flanks answering the enemy's heavy batteries. Its embankments remain full formed — high and steep; the interior cut up by ridges of traverses protecting from flank fire, and the bottom gashed with the cavernous bomb-proofs making thick cover from the terrific work of great guns and mortars all through the dreary siege — looking now like the underground best-dens of the old Roman Coliseum. Grown over now — the whole of it — with trees so thick and dark and somber, and casting so gloomy a shade down among the strange pits and dens, I almost shuddered even at the shadow of the scenes enacted here in that year of tragedy, and wondered deeply how the men kept their cheer, as the brave hearts did.

Out in the open front are the hedge-marked lines of low parapet and rifle-pits of our advanced infantry and out-lying pickets — though some are close under the guns of the fort. The ditches are still so sharp we would not drive over them with safety to our carriage, but had to dismount and climb across, pushing our way through the dense hedge. On the smooth slopes between the two opposing lines, the rank broom-sedge, leg-deep, softly waving; here and there little garden-beds of richer shrubbery, where the ever-living spirit has transfigured immortal blood.

Passing across the slight valley to the enemy's works, we found them also in good form. My guide assured me they were now little changed from their old appearance as on the day of our assault. He added that the Confederates regarded this as the strongest part of their lines. It was easy to trace the entrenchments of the infantry — Kershaw's Mississippians, Georgians and South Carolinians, and on their right some of our old Alabama friends — companions of the symposium at Round Top the year before, troops of Longstreet's Corps who had come up early in the evening before, and taken the place of Johnson's Division there — not less than five thousand men behind those entrenchments. At close intervals are the heavier works, the places of their guns telling no uncertain story.

Consulting the worn Confederate war map of that date I had taken along, the old muniments were readily identified, and the record of their power applied to the justification of memory. At the redan in front, five guns; in the two lunettes right and left, seven guns each; behind the interval, in a retired work, four guns. Twenty-three guns, then, opposite our advance, where we were to pass through the cross fire of the entrenched infantry, and carry the guns at the bayonet point. Moreover, four hundred yards to their right, (our left), across the Plank Road, Fort Mahone, its seven great guns enfilading every inch of our advance from beginning to end — and the end so dark, foreordained, and to me, at least, foreknown. I could see now how well based that foreknowledge was.

Crossing the little run in front, which showed me where I fell, I came upon a little bunch of sassafras bushes, rather lavishly nourished, it seemed, and I cut one of them to serve, like pansies — "for thoughts." Doing this, I saw a bullet point sticking up out of the ground, and stooping to pick this up, others came to view. Without moving more than a step, I picked up four more minie-balls, a pistol bullet, and a Union officer's vest-button.

Some good angel was near again, for a young girl came out from the Rives house a little behind the line of works, and not far from my last position picked up a fragment of shrapnel with two lead bullets still held fast in the iron band. This with native grace, or instinctive recognition, she handed me; and I was moved to give her in return a fair-sized piece of silver, in token of her ministry and of my thanksgiving that I did not get it otherwise — the shell I mean — when I was younger. But all that has passed — let it pass now.

Regretting that my visit could not extend for five miles further leftward along the lines where so many engagements costly but fruitless had ensanguined the history of every corps and battery of our army, especially the ground of the splendid charge of our Sixth Corps, carrying the defenses of Petersburg, we returned towards the town, passing the somber grove which now covers the "crater" of so sad a story where after the explosion of the mine, our assaulting columns instead of seizing the moment of the enemy's confusion to rush them through into the town, were led into the smoking crater itself, there to huddle under storms of shrapnel and canister, till forced to give up and get back — those who could — and let the enemy sit down there and count the hecatombs of dead. This monument also remains — dark, deep-cut intaglio. To us it speaks only of gloom — skilled plan, long toil, brave endeavor, made fruitless through lack of grip and grit on the part of intermediate commanders.

Then turning, we peacefully entered that once so longingly beheld, long waited for, long fought for city; now so prosperous so bright, so beautiful. Now as then, city of churches and schools; the roofs and spires still as we saw then shining in morning or sunset light, so graceful, so sweet, so heaven-pointing — so hell-surrounded!

Wrapped in these reflections, the shadow of that whole, dark campaign of 1864 came over me — which up to that June day had cost our army seventy thousand men. Then I was nearing the crest of manhood, where

NARA

Petersburg, Virginia, c. 1861-1865

life looks back and forward — the middle-point of our allotted years — but it seemed that experience was at the climax. I remember how often in those days stole over my spirit that mood of Dante, at the beginning of the "Inferno," which I give you in his own deep-echoing words:

Ned Mezzo del camin di nostra vita,
Mi retrovai per una selva oscura
Che la diritta via era smaritta.

[Midway the path of life,
I found myself in a gloomy wood,
where the right way out was perplexed.]

You were younger yet, I take it, my Companions — in the flower of youth, or to change the figure, in the border-land of manhood, the testing ground of the knighthood which you won. By what crucial tests, through what ordeals of initiation, you passed to that high degree! Far deeper yours than those of the days of chivalry; the old investiture of knighthood — the searching purifications, the fastings and prayer, the day and night prostrations before the altar whereon the sword was laid, all the self-renouncing symbols of the "vigil of arms." And then the consummate salutation — the accolade, the crowning stroke on the shoulder; theirs, with the flat of the sword — yours with the fiery edge!

The heroism of those earlier days was personal, it is said. Was it otherwise than personal — yours? The story of that ancient chivalry lives ever in romantic song. Where is the minstrelsy of yours?

On my return to Petersburg, I found myself among friends. The old Confederate officers in the city were gathered in force to greet my coming. And strong, manly men they were. Nothing could exceed their heartiness and hospitality. They opened for the occasion their hall of war records and relics, where we talked over the feats and defeats of many an old field. In the evening there was a symposium, where our various experiences and different views of things give spice to comradeship.

Perhaps the most striking attention received was that of an old Confederate from the ranks, who was at Rives' Salient on that dark June day of the bloody years, and who was as badly cut up with wounds as any man I ever saw alive. Our interview was both sharpened and deepened by our reciprocal experiences on that mortal day....

APPENDIX B

[EXCERPT OF A LETTER FROM JOSHUA LAWRENCE CHAMBERLAIN TO SARAH BRASTOW CHAMBERLAIN FARRINGTON, CHAMBERLAIN COLLECTION, SPECIAL COLLECTIONS, FOGLER LIBRARY, UNIVERSITY OF MAINE AT ORONO]

Washington 29 Jan 1882

[Salutation] My dear Sister;

...Friday I visited the battle fields of Petersburg & spent 4 hours in trying to identify the spot where I fell on the 18th of June 64 in leading a charge upon the Rebel works. All is changed there now. What was a solid piece of woods through which I led my troops is now all cleared field, & the hill side so smooth there is now grown up with little clumps of trees — marking some spots made more rich perhaps by the bloody struggles enacted on them. At last, guided by the rail road cut & the well remembered direction of the church spires of the city, I found the spot — or a space of 20 or 30 feet within which I must have fallen. It is now a plowed field — too rich, I suppose since the 18 of June to be left barren by the owner — & there are in it the remnants of a last years corn field.

Standing & musing there remembering how I thought of Mother in that calm ebbing away of life amidst the horrible carnage, I looked down & saw a bullet & while stooping to pick it up, another & another appeared in sight & I took up six within as many feet of each other and of the spot where I fell. You may imagine what the havoc must have been that day.

And for 17 years relic hunters have been carrying away lead & iron from the field — amounting, I was told, to cart-loads. I could easily no doubt have found many more had I searched, or kicked away the earth a little — But these I have, & that other that made so straight a way through me, will do.

You can not imagine, I believe, what thought came over me, as I thought of all those who stood there on that day — for & against — & what it was all for, & what would come of it — & of those who on one side & the other thought there was something at stake worthy of dearest sacrifice.

Such thought never would end, had one time to ponder, & it is well perhaps that the common cares & inexorable duties of life call us away from too long thoughts...

APPENDIX C

Lines before Petersburg
June 18, 1864

I have just received a verbal order not through the usual channels, but by a staff-officer unknown to me, purporting to come from the General commanding the Army, directing me to assault the main works of the enemy in my front.

Circumstances lead me to believe the General cannot be perfectly aware of my situation, which has greatly changed within the last hour. I have just carried a crest, an advanced post occupied by the enemy's artillery supported by infantry. I am advanced a mile beyond our own lines, and in an isolated position. On my right a deep railroad cut; my left flank in the air, with no support whatever. In my front at close range is a strongly entrenched line of infantry and artillery, with projecting salients right and left such that my advance would be swept by a cross-fire, while a large fort to my left enfilades my entire advance, [as I experienced in carrying this position.] In the hollow along my front close up to the enemy's works, appears to be bad ground, swampy, boggy, where my men would be held at great disadvantage under destructive fire.

I have got up three batteries and am placing them on the reverse slope of this crest to enable me to hold against expected attack. To leave these guns behind me unsupported, their retreat cut off by the railroad cut, would expose them to loss in case of our repulse. Fully aware of the responsibility I take I beg to be assured that the order to attack with my single brigade is with the General's full understanding. I have here a veteran brigade of six regiments; and my responsibility for these men warrants [????] in wishing assurance that no mistake in communicating orders compels me to sacrifice them.

From what I can see of the enemy's lines, it is my opinion that if an assault is to be made, it should be by nothing less than the whole army.

Very respectfully,
Joshua L. Chamberlain
Colonel commanding
1st Brigade 1st Division
5th Corps

[Transcribed from the original, as reproduced in "The Hero of Gettysburg," *Lewiston Journal*, September 1-6, 1900.]

NOTES

INTRODUCTION

1. Joshua Laurence Chamberlain (JLC) Service Record, NA. In early October 1863, Chamberlain served on a court martial board, a duty often reserved for ailing officers. Thomas P. Lowry, The Index Project, October 1, 1863, File Numbers 11980, 11987, 11378, February 1, 1864, 11303, 11372. On October 16, 1863, Ellis Spear of the 20th Maine recorded that the "Col." was sick in camp and traveling in an ambulance. Ellis Spear, *Civil War Recollections of General Ellis Spear* (Orono: University of Maine Press, 1997) 227-28; JLC Service & Medical Records, NA; JLC Letterbook, Pejepscot Historical Society, Brunswick, Maine, 39; Jack Walsh, M.D., *Medical Histories of Union Generals* (Kent, OH: Kent State Press, 1996) 63.

2. Grant was appointed General in Chief on March 12, 1864. JLC to Deborah Folsom, March 12, 1864, Noble Papers, Specials Collections Library, Duke University; JLC to Deborah Folsom, April 14, 1864, Maine Historical Society; JLC to E.D. Townsend, 25 Apr. 1864, DU; Frances Adams Chamberlain to Deborah Folsom, n.d. [early May 1864], Maine Historical Society; Mark M. Boatner, *The Civil War Dictionary* (New York: Vintage Books, 1991) 48; Noah Brooks, Washington D.C., in Lincoln's Time (Athens: The University of Georgia Press, 1989) 137-38. *OR* XXXVI, I, 125, 133. Regarding the accuracy of 5th Corps casualty returns, see Morris Schaff, *The Battle of the Wilderness* (Boston: Houghton Mifflin, 1910) 210.

3. See William Steere's, *The Wilderness Campaign* (Harrisburg, PA: Stackpole, 1960) and William Matter's, *If It Takes All Summer* (Chapel Hill: University of North Carolina, 1988), still the best and most balanced accounts of the battles. The diary of William Livermore, a 20th Maine soldier in a Washington hospital, states that Chamberlain left the capitol on May 16 [Livermore Diary, Special Collections, University of Maine at Orono]. The diary of Ellis Spear, then acting commander of the 20th Maine, muddies the waters regarding the date of Chamberlain's return to the army, stating that JLC returned on May 15 [Spear, 109, 242]. But Chamberlain consistently dates his return to the army as May 18. JLC, Letterbook, PHS 45, 39; JLC to Governor Cony, May 18, 1864, Maine State Archives. The regiments in JLC's command for this night advance were the 20th Maine, 1st, 4th, and 16th Michigan, 18th Massachusetts, 44th New York, 83rd and 118th Pennsylvania. Of those regiments involved, unit reports, accounts, and other sources indicate that the movement Chamberlain commanded was made on the night of May 17-18, rather than the night of May 18-19. [Eugene Nash, *A History of the Forty-fourth Regiment New York Volunteer Infantry in the Civil War* (Dayton: Morningside, 1988 reprint 1910 edition) 192; Spear, 110, 243; John L. Parker, *History of the Twenty-Second Massachusetts Infantry, the Second Co. Sharpshooters, and the Third Light Battery* (Boston: The Regimental Association, 1887) 444; Washington A. Roebling, "Report, May 4 to Aug. 20, 1864"; Gouverneur K. Warren Papers, New York State Library, 45-46; Andrew A. Humphreys, *The Virginia Campaign of '64 and '65: The Army of the Potomac and the Army of the James* (New York: Charles Scribner's

Sons, 1883) 109-110; Powell, 651-52; *OR* XXXVI, I, 577, 581; *OR* XXXVI, II, 821, 847] Hancock and Wright's May 18 assault was made against "Lee's Final Line," the enemy fortifications built to stop that 2nd and 6th Corps' May 12 attack. The ill-planned, but fortuitous Federal advance on May 12 [see Matter, 183-268, 302-312] may be considered a Union victory in terms of enemy guns and prisoners taken [eighteen to twenty guns and 3,000 prisoners], with 2,000 to 3,000 Confederate casualties. But the high number of Federal casualties [7,000] and the fact that the breach in the Rebel line was ultimately repaired by leaving the salient to the attackers make it a costly victory of dubious military value. General Bartlett's indisposition is unknown, but we may speculate that a severe fall he took with his horse at the Wilderness may have triggered one of the frequent attacks of rheumatism with which he suffered throughout the war. Theodore Gerrish, *Army Life: A Private's Reminiscences of the War* (Portland, ME: Hoyt, Fogg, & Donham, 1882) 168-69; Walsh, 21.

4. Humphreys, 119-123; Matter, 317-29, 331-38, 348. Grant, in his memoir [239-40], credits the 2nd Corps with coming to the aid of General Robert O. Tyler's newly arrived, untrained heavy artillery units, which had checked Ewell's attack on the Federal right. But Roebling, General Warren's aide who was on the spot, states that only the 5th Corps' Maryland Brigade became engaged in support of the artillerymen. Roebling, 48-55. Adam Badeau, *Grant's military secretary, in his Military History of Ulysses S. Grant* (New York: C. Appleton & Co., 1885, II) 208, accuses Warren of failing to fall upon Ewell's flank as ordered with his remaining divisions. But Griffin's, Robinson's, and Cutler's Divisions were stretched thin to hold the 5th Corps line, and the records contain no such order. Badeau also fails to acknowledge the Rebel diversionary attack sent against the right of the 5th Corps line during Ewell's assault. *OR* XXXVI, II 916-7, 925. Four streams, the Mat, Ta, Po and Ni merged to form the Mattaponi River. Nash, 192-3; Michael J. Miller, *The North Anna Campaign: "Even to Hell Itself"* (Lynchburg: H.E. Howard, 1989) 4, 25-27, 31-33, 37-43; *OR*, XXXVI, III, 55, 64-5; *OR* XXXVI, I, 140, 149, 582. While many perceive the 2nd and 6th Corps bore the brunt of the fighting at Spotsylvania with their operations on May 10, 12, and 18, casualty figures for the entire battle show that 5th Corps action on May 8 and 9, as well as repeated reconnaissances in force swelled Warren's losses beyond that of the 6th Corps. Aggregate losses at Spotsylvania were: 2nd Corps, 6,642; 5th Corps, 4,480; 6th Corps, 4,042. *OR* XXXVI, I, 140, 144, 146; Steere [p. 463] estimates Confederate losses at the Wilderness at 8,700. Matter [p. 348] estimates Confederate losses at Spotsylvania at between 9,000 and 10,000.

5. Grant, 243; Miller, 3-5, 12-36; Matter, 343; Stephen Z. Starr, *The Union Cavalry in the Civil War* (Baton Rouge: Louisiana State University Press, 1981) II, 96-97, 115. Sheridan, setting out on May 9 with nearly 10,000 men, left behind only dismounted cavalrymen and 600 wounded. Humphreys, 120-25.

6. Miller, 23-24, 44. Unit histories and reports indicate that 5th Corps' infantry encountered Rebel cavalry only. Roebling, 54-57; Roger D. Hunt, *Brevet Brigadier Generals in Blue* (Gaithersburg, MD: Olde Soldiers Books, 1990) 486; Frederick Phisterer, *New York in the War of the Rebellion* (Albany: J.B. Lyon Co., 3rd Edition, vol. 1, 1912) 875-76. The Telegraph Road was so named because telegraph wires

from Fredericksburg ran alongside the road. *OR* XXXVI, I, 582; *OR* XXXVI, III, 88, 90-91, 98-99; Spear, 244. Though Sheridan did not even know the whereabouts of his own army, he inadvertently played a small role in the action. While awaiting supplies at the White House on the Pamunkey before the cavalry's return to the AoP, he sent General George Custer's Cavalry Brigade out to destroy bridges over the South Anna and to disrupt Lee's communications. Custer actually occupied Hanover Court House on May 20, destroying several Virginia Central Railroad bridges and a mile of track, but Breckinridge's arrival, bolstering the Rebel cavalry, denied Custer entry to the all-important Hanover Junction and forced him to withdraw. Humphreys, 124-26.

7. *OR*, XXXVI, III, 53-59, 83-85, 88, 90-91, 93; Miller, 5, 40, 42; Clifford Dowdey, *The Wartime Papers of R.E. Lee* (New York: Bramhall House, 1961) 746-47.

8. Survivors' Association, *History of the Corn Exchange Regiment 118th Pennsylvania Volunteers* (Philadelphia: J.L. Smith, 1888) 436-37; Miller, 44-45; *OR* XXXVI, I, 585, 592; Boatner, 136. John R. Chambliss [1853 USMA], a veteran Confederate cavalry officer, had won command of Rooney Lee's former brigade, the 9th, 10th and 13th Virginia Cavalry Regiments. [Miller, 13-14, 28, 31-32] Chambliss was killed at Deep Bottom in August 1864. *OR* XXXVI, I, 582. A. M. Judson, *History of the Eighty-third Regiment Pennsylvania Volunteers* (Erie: B.F.H. Lynn Publisher, nd) 99. Judson asserts that the 83rd fought with or supported the 16th Michigan on the 5th Corps' front, and contrary to JLC's notes regarding his commands, Judson also asserts that the 44th New York took part in JLC's flanking movement. JLC, Letterbook, 2, 45; Roebling, 58-9.

9. 118th Pennsylvania, 437-38; JLC, Letterbook, 39-40.

10. Miller, 15; *OR* XXXVI, III, 80-82, 88-89, 92, 116-19, 125-31; Roebling, 58-61; Humphreys, 127-28; *OR* XXXVI, I, 583; O.B. Curtis, *History of the Twenty-fourth Michigan of the Iron Brigade* (Detroit: Winn & Hammond, 1891) 250; Curtis, Roebling, Humphreys, Swinton, Gerrish, Buell, and the 118th unit history all credit Bartlett's 3rd Brigade as being the first to wade the river. William Swinton, *Campaigns of the Army of the Potomac* (New York: Charles Scribner's Sons, 1882, Revised & Reissued) 473; Gerrish, 191; August Buell, "The Cannoneer" (Washington: *The National Tribune*, 1890). But two 3rd Brigade historians, Nash & Judson, state that Sweitzer's 2nd Brigade, 1st Division, crossed first, as does Parker's and a number of 2nd Brigade histories, Daniel Macnamara, *The History of the Ninth Regiment Massachusetts Volunteer Infantry* (Boston: E.B. Stillings, 1899); Francis J. Parker, *The Story of the 32nd Regiment Massachusetts Infantry* (Boston: C.W. Alkins, 1880). It is possible that this confusion arises in part because the 22nd Massachusetts [2nd Brigade] acted as Griffin's skirmishers this day, and may have crossed with or before the 3rd Brigade. John Parker and Robert Carter's, *Four Brothers in Blue* (Austin: University of Texas, 1978 reprint) 406-7, 429. One 3rd Brigade report also states that they formed their battle line in the rear of the 2nd Brigade. But if we consider what time units report crossing the river, most accounts seem to indicate that the 3rd Brigade crossed before the 2nd. *OR* XXXVI, I, 563, 582, 585, 587; *OR* XXXVI, III, 825.

11. *OR* XXXVI, III, 118-19, 125-26, 128-29, 157, 825; Edward Porter Alexander, *Military Memoirs of a Confederate* (New York: Charles Scribner's Sons, 1907) 531;

Miller, 63; Roebling, 61-62; Allan Nevins, *Diary of Battle: The Personal Journals of Colonel Charles S. Wainwright* (New York, Harcourt, Brace & World, 1962) 385; Nash, 194; *OR* XXXVI, III, 128-29; 118th Pennsylvania, 444. George W. Carleton to A.B. Farwell, January 8, 1866, Frost Family Papers, Manuscripts & Archives Library, Yale University. While in one set of his notes, Chamberlain lists the 20th Maine as his sole command on this date, in other notes, he lists his command on May 23 as the 20th Maine, the 44th New York, and the 83rd Pennsylvania. JLC Letterbook, 2, 45. Ellis Spear's diary indicates that Spear had command of the 20th Maine during the advance toward the front. Spears, 114, 244. It also seems from the unit histories of the regiments involved, that Chamberlain was in error regarding the 83rd Pennsylvania, which, along with the 1st Michigan, was sent to Sweitzer's right, while the 44th New York and 118th Pennsylvania were sent to the left with the 20th Maine. Judson, 100; *OR* XXXVI, I, 76-77.

12. Dowdey, 739; Humphreys, 130-33; Roebling, 64-65; Miller, 93-94. Chamberlain paid tribute to the gallant Captain Phillips in an oration, "The Grand Review," saying, "And here the 5th Massachusetts which wrought miracles of valor all the way from the Fifth Corps' right, across the valley of death at Gettysburg, to the North Anna; where, planted in my very skirmish line, Phillips, erect on the gun-carriage, launched percussion into buildings full of sharpshooters picking off my best men." *"Bayonet! Forward"* (Gettysburg: Stan Clark Military Books, 1994) 175; *OR* XXXVI, III, 145, 149, 157-59, 165, 169.

13. Roebling, 65-66; *OR* XXXVI, III, 190-94, 206-7; Nash, 194-95; Humphreys, 133. Sheridan's cavalry having at last returned to the Army of the Potomac, the cavalry expedition was commanded by General James H. Wilson. Chamberlain recorded that the 20th Maine was engaged at "Noel's Turn." Presumably, JLC referred to the 3rd Brigade's passing of Noel's Turn on the 24th and movement toward Anderson's on the 25th. JLC, Letterbook, 3, 45; The One Hundred Fifty-fifth Regimental Association, *Under the Maltese Cross (Campaigns 155th Pennsylvania Regiment)* (Pittsburgh: The Werner Co., 1910) 167. Washington Roebling, a graduate of Rensselaer Polytechnic Institute of Troy, New York, had been with Warren on Little Round Top at Gettysburg, served as an engineer officer on Warren's staff until the end of the war, and was promoted to colonel for gallant conduct.

14. Chamberlain records that he had command of the 20th Maine, 44th New York, 1st and 16th Michigan, 83rd and 118th Pennsylvania, and 18th Massachusetts. JLC, Letterbook, 2, 4; Nash, 194-95; Roebling, 66-68; Curtis, 252; *OR* XXXVI, I, 578; 118th, 446-47; *OR* XXXVI, I, 578; Humphreys, 160-61; Spear, 115, 245-46; C.W. Owen, *The First Michigan Infantry; Three Months and Three Years* (Quincy Herald Print), entry for May 26, 1864; Miller, 128-29, 136; Dowdey, 751-53.

15. Humphreys, 161-66; Wainwright, 389-91; 118th, 447; Roebling, 68.

16. Humphreys, 166-68; Roebling, 69-71; *OR* XXXVI, III 335-37, 348, 395. General Richard S. Ewell being ill, his 2nd Corps was under the command of Gen. Jubal Early. *OR* XXXVI, I, 1074.

17. JLC, Letterbook, 2, 45. Chamberlain listed his commands on May 30 at Magnolia Swamp as 20th Maine, 44th New York, 1st and 16th Michigan, 18th abd 29th Massachusetts, 83rd and 118th Pennsylvania. The 29th Massachusetts, formerly of the 9th Corps, on its return to the front at this time was assigned to the 3rd Bri-

gade, 5th Corps. They were displeased with this arrangement, and were eventually sent back to Burnside. William Osborne, *The History of the Twenty-ninth Regiment of Massachusetts Volunteer Infantry* (Boston: Albert J. Wright, 1877) 298; *OR* XXXVI, I, 592; George C. Hopper, *First Michigan Infantry: Three Months and Three Years* (Coldwater Courier Print, 1891) 16; Owen, entry for May 30; Judson, 102; Roebling, 70-73; Humphreys, 168-71; *OR* XXXVI, I, 585; *OR* XXXVI, III, 340-42, 348, 351, 361. Crawford's Brigade was made up almost entirely of the men of the Pennsylvania Reserves, whose terms of enlistment ended the next day. Charles E. Davis, *Three Years in the Army: The Story of the Thirteenth Massachusetts Volunteers* (Boston: Estes and Lauriat, 1894) 353. General Henry H. Lockwood had just assumed command of Robinson's 2nd Division. General Torbert, though he would insist that he had troopers on the left of the 5th Corps all day, was in action at Old Church, driving the enemy toward Cold Harbor. Chamberlain Association, "Joshua Lawrence Chamberlain; A Sketch" 38-39 [copies at the Bangor Public Library and PHS].

18. Roebling, 73; Humphreys, 170-75; JLC, Letterbook, 45; Judson, 104; 118th, 45.

19. Humphreys, 173-76; JLC, Letterbook, 45; Roebling, 74-75; *OR* XXXVI, III, 446-49, 450-51, 453-54, 459; Judson, 102; Nash, 199; *OR* XXXVI, I, 578, 583, 586, 592; Gerrish, 193; Osborne, 299; Grant, 265-66. Many mistakes and miscalculations had been made during June 1, but Grant, curiously, would reserve special criticism for Warren. Ignoring the wooded swamps on Warren's front [so aptly described by Grant on page 258 of his *Memoirs*], and the enemy's assaults that were made on the 5th Corps during the day, Grant wrote, "...soon after light on the 1st of June, Anderson, who commanded the corps on Lee's left, was seen moving along Warren's front. Warren was ordered to attack him vigorously in flank, while Wright was directed to move out and get on his front. Warren fired his artillery at the enemy; but lost so much time in making ready that the enemy got by, and at three o'clock he reported the enemy was strongly entrenched in his front, and besides his line were so long that he had no mass of troops to move with. He seemed to have forgotten that lines in rear of an army hold themselves while their defenders are fighting in their front." One is reminded of Hancock's observations at Petersburg when he found himself in much the same position as Warren had on June 1-3. With the 2nd Corps holding a long line confronting well-manned Rebel earthworks, when ordered by Meade to prepare for an assault at dawn on June 18, Hancock replied, "In making arrangements for an assault I find that about all of my command is in line, and where it cannot be withdrawn. To assault at a given point I can probably get three, perhaps four, lines, with a brigade front. I cannot attack with the rest of my force, except in case of decided success by this assaulting column, as in case of repulse I would have nothing to hold my line. I will assault with the force indicated, as I do not understand that you intend any part of my line abandoned or compromised, except the enemy show evident signs of weakness." [XL, II, 163]

20. Humphreys, 176-82; Roebling, 79-81; *OR* XXXVI, III, 478, 482-83, 486-91, 496, 499-500, 676; 118th, 455-59; Carleton, 7-8. It is estimated that besides killed and wounded, 400 1st Division men were taken prisoner during the initial Rebel attack. Grant, 268.

21. Roebling, 81-84 ; *OR* XXXVI, III, 493-94, 536-38, 543; Grant, 268; Humphreys, 182-89; Nathan S. Clark Diary, Maine State Archives, 72.

22. Roebling, 85-89; *OR* XXXVI, III, 609-10, 612-13, 627-28, 631, 652; Spear, 118-20, 248; JLC to John Chamberlain, December 19, 1864, Chamberlain Collection, Special Collections Library, Bowdoin College. JLC, Letterbook, 45, Richard E. Matthews, *The One Hundred Forty-ninth Pennsylvania Volunteer Infantry Unit in the Civil War* (Jefferson, North Carolina, 1994) 168. On June 6, Warren wrote to General Griffin, "I wish you would make out a recommendation for the promotion of Colonel Chamberlain. I will forward it at once, so that it can take its chance with some others that are going to be forwarded." General Bartlett, the 3rd Brigade commander, also wrote a letter of recommendation for Chamberlain's promotion. *OR* XXXVI, III, 652; Joseph J. Bartlett to General S. Williams, June 6, 1864, JLC Service Record, NA.

23. Roebling, 88-89; Wainwright, 407-8; *OR* XXXVI, III, 649-52, 655, 657-58, 674-75; Thomas Chamberlain, *History of the One Hundred and Fiftieth Regiment Pennsylvania Volunteers, Second Regiment, Bucktail Brigade* (Baltimore: Butternut & Blue reprint, 1986) 259; Robert Tilney, *My Life in the Army: Three Years and a Half with the Fifth Army Corps* (Philadelphia: Ferris & Leach, 1912) 86. Four brigades under General Robert F. Hoke captured the Federal garrison at Plymouth, North Carolina in April 1864. James M. Gibbs, *History of the First Battalion Pennsylvania Six Months Volunteers & 187th Regiment Pennsylvania Volunteer Infantry* (Harrisburg: Survivors' Association, 1905) 85-86.

24. Tilney, 87; Humphreys, 194-99; Grant, 284. The AoJ expedition was under the command of General Quincy Adams Gillmore, 10th Corps, who, deeming the Petersburg works too strong, returned to Bermuda Hundred without attacking. *OR* XXXVI, III, 745, 747, 750.

25. Roebling, 92-93; *OR* XXXVI, III, 763; *OR* XL, II, 6; Chamberlain, 259; Gibbs, 86-89. Wilson's was the only cavalry division to act as the eyes and ears of the army. On June 7, Sheridan, with his other two divisions, was leading an ill-fated expedition to unite with General David Hunter at Charlottesville, Virginia. Humphreys, 194-96, 230-35. Though Sheridan, as was his habit, puts the best face upon his cavalry's actions for the period of June 7-13, one need not even read between the lines of his own report to see that his expedition failed. *OR* XXXVI, I, 784-86.

26. Roebling, 93-95; *OR* XL, I, 453; *OR* XL, II, 6, 8, 11-12, 31-32 [Crawford's June 13 dispatches, pp. 31-32, misdated June 14]; Dowdey, 777; Edward Porter Alexander, *The Personal Recollections of General Edward Porter Alexander* (Chapel Hill: University of North Carolina Press, 1989) 420. For a description of the advantages of Warren's position at White Oak Swamp, see Humphreys, 199-202.

27. Gibbs, 89-90; Chamberlain, 259; Survivors Association, *History of the 121st Regiment Pennsylvania Volunteers* (Philadelphia: Press of Burk & McFetridge Co., 1893) 78; Roebling, 95-96; Wainwright, 418; Theodore Lyman, "Army of the Potomac, June 5-15, 1864" (Papers of the Military Historical Society of Massachusetts, vol. V) 22. Lyman reported that the pontoon bridge across the James was 2,000 feet long, thirteen feet wide, using ninety-two boats and braced by three schooners. It took ten hours to construct, and half the infantry, 4,000 cavalry and the train of wagons and artillery, which was thirty-five miles long, all crossed the pontoon in

forty-eight hours. *OR* XL, 1, 167, 303, 314-15; William A. Frassanito, *Grant & Lee: The Virginia Campaigns* (New York: Scribner's Sons, 1983) 205-7; Grant, 293-94, 574. Thomas J. Howe, *Wasted Valor: The Petersburg Campaign June 15-18* (Lynchburg, VA: H.E. Howard, Inc. 1988) intro, 19-36; *OR* XL, II, 36, 60-61; 72-73, 75; [Pierre] G.T. Beauregard, "Letter of General G.T. Beauregard to General C.M. Wilcox" (Papers of the Military Historical Society of Massachusetts, vol. V) pp. 119-120; *OR* XL, I, 303-5. General Meade would state, "Had Major-General Hancock and myself been apprised in time of the contemplated movement against Petersburg, and the necessity of his cooperation, I am of the opinion he could have been pushed much earlier to the scene of operations, but as matters occurred and with our knowledge of them I do not see how any censure can be attached to General Hancock and his corps." Hancock, feeling that undue blame was being placed upon the 2nd Corps, would request an investigation. Grant would reply to Meade, "I am very much mistaken if you were not informed of the contemplated movement against Petersburg as soon as I returned to Wilcox's Landing from Bermuda Hundred, and that the object of getting the 2nd Corps up without waiting for the supply train to come up to issue rations to them, was that they might be on hand if required." Grant refused Hancock's request for an inquiry, commenting, "No investigation can now be had without great prejudice to the service, nor do I think an investigation necessary at any time."

28.   Dowdey, 776-90. Special mention should be made of Col. George H. Chapman and his 2nd Brigade of Wilson's Division. Although they bore the brunt of the cavalry fight at White Oak Swamp, Chapman would also perform outstanding duty on June 14 and 15, deflecting Rebel probes and gathering hard information on the position and movements of the enemy. *OR* XL, II, 11-12, 34-36, 70-72. Interestingly, Lee's only major movement on June 15 had nothing to do with his concerns regarding the AoP. Early, now permanently in command of Ewell's Corps, marched away from the ANV on the morning of June 15. Sent initially to confront Federal General Hunter's expedition and its approach to Lynchburg, Early would later enter the Shenandoah Valley, where he would, in the weeks and months to come, provide some major headaches for the Federals. Beauregard, "Letter," 120; *OR* XL, I, 167, 306.

29.   *OR* XL, I, 167-68, 453; *121st*, 78; Gibbs, 90; Chamberlain, 260; Roebling, 97-98; JLC, Letterbook, 45; XL, II, 94-95, 114-15; Matthews, 179-80. After his arrival at Petersburg at 2 p.m. on June 16, Meade countermanded Butler's orders to have Gen. August Kautz's cavalry return to the Army of the James. Kautz picketed the AoP's left until the 5th Corps' arrival late that night. Sheridan on this day had proceeded from White House as far as Guiney's Bridge, seeking supplies for his hungry troopers and their mounts. Wilson was still protecting the AoP's trains at the James River crossing. *OR* XXXVI, I, 784; XL, II, 140; Wainwright, 422.

30.   Roebling, 97; *OR* XL, I, 167-68, 306-7; XL, II, 87-89, 94, 113, 117-18.

Barnard and Comstock must either have been unaware of or chose not to consider the opinion of cavalry commander General Kautz. Stationed on the AoP's left, Kautz felt that the unmanned Rebel defense to the left of Hancock and Burnside was the weakest point in the enemy line. George R. Agassiz, ed., *Meade's Headquarters 1863-1865: Letters of Colonel Theodore Lyman from the Wilderness to Appomattox* (Boston: The Atlantic Monthly Press, 1922) 165.

31. *OR* XL, II, 87, 101, 117-18, 122, 125-26, 128-38, 141-44, 146, 148, 151-53, 154-55; Dowdey, 787. Efforts by the 6th and 18th Corps to swap positions certainly limited the efficiency and availability of both corps on June 17. And when the 6th Corps division that was to have relieved Smith failed to appear, a division from the 5th Corps, and even one from the embattled 9th Corps, were considered as relief for Smith. Author's note: It should be remembered that this was well before the days of daylight savings time [DST], and darkness fell around 8 p.m. in June in Virginia.

32. Roebling, 98-102; *OR* XL, II, 118-19, 123, 126-28, 133, 136-38, 156, 178. Before news of the Federal withdrawal became known at army headquarters, Meade, in a mood of optimism, sent an aide to Grant with news of the AoP's attacks. Several hours later, Grant replied from his City Point headquarters, "The news is good and I hope efforts in the morning will improve it." He also gave Meade permission to retain Smith's 18th Corps for the next day's assault. Amazingly, there is evidence that as late as the morning of June 18, reliable telegraphic communication had not been established between Meade's and Grant's headquarters.

33. Dowdey, 784-91; [Pierre] G.T. Beauregard, "Four Days Battle at Petersburg" *Battles and Leaders of the Civil War* (New York: Century, 1884, 1888, vol. IV) 543; Mac Wycoff, *A History of the Second South Carolina Infantry: 1861-65* (Fredericksburg: Sergeant Kirkland's Museum and Historical Society, 1994) 130-31; Beauregard, "Letter," 120-23; Hagood, 268, 280; *OR* XL, I, 757; XL, II, 160-61, 668. Beauregard's defensive line had retired toward Petersburg, but at Rives' Salient, the new Confederate line which would be known as the Harris Line, joined the original Dimmock Line fortifications. Lacking other sources of information, Meade placed great importance on the reports of the AoP provost marshal. Determining what commands enemy prisoners and deserters came from provided some means of determining what and whose forces he faced. But even though ANV reinforcements had poured into Petersburg throughout the day and been safely positioned, by the night of June 18, the Federal provost marshal was still reporting that all Rebel prisoners were coming only from Beauregard's force.

CHARGE AT FORT HELL

2. JLC service record, NA; *OR* XXXVI, III, 652; JLC, Letterbook, Pejepscot Historical Society, 39, 44-45; Eugene Nash, *A History of the 44th Regiment New York Volunteer Infantry* (Chicago: R.R. Donnelley & Sons, 1911) 161-62, 164; Maine Adjutant General's Report, I,1864-65, 332; "Narrow Escape" and "Casualties in the Maine Twentieth," clippings in John Chamberlain's Diary, PHS; Ellis Spear, *The Civil War Recollections of General Ellis Spear* (Orono: University of Maine Press, 1997) 47, 222, 227-28; JLC Medical Records, NA; George Adams Diaries, December 18, 1863, First Parish Church, Brunswick, Maine; Frances Adams Chamberlain to Deborah Folsom, n.d. [early May, 1864] Maine Historical Society, JLC to Col. E.D. Townsend, April 25, 1864, William H. Noble Papers, Special Collections Library, Duke University; JLC to Col. E.D. Townsend, May 9, 1864, NA; William Livermore Diary, Special Collections, Fogler Library, University of Maine, Orono, Maine; Mark M. Boatner, *Civil War Dictionary* (New York: Vintage Books, 1991) 48; Jack Walsh, *Medical Histories of Union Generals Kent* (Ohio: Kent State University Press, 1996) 21.

3.   *OR* XXXIII, 722-23; *OR* XXXVI, III, 652; *OR* XXVII, 156, 174, 253, 256, 337, 342, 347;
     Stewart Sifakis, *Who Was Who in the Union* (New York: Facts on File, 1988) 345; *OR*,
     XL, III, 520-21; James M. Gibbs, *History of the First Battalion Pennsylvania Six Month
     Volunteers and 187th Regiment Pennsylvania Volunteer Infantry* (Survivors' Associa-
     tion, 1905) 18-20, 77, 79, 83.
4.   Richard Wayne Lykes, *Campaign for Petersburg* (Washington: U.S. Government Print-
     ing Office, National Park Service History Series, 1970) 7-10; R.A. Brock, *Southern
     Historical Society Papers* (Richmond: 1907) XXXV, 9, 14-15; Beauregard, 119-23;
     Johnson Hagood, *Memoirs of the War of the Secession* (Columbia, South Carolina:
     The State Co., 1910) 265-68; John F. Glenn, "Brave Defense of the Cockade City,"
     Southern Historical Society Paper (Richmond: Published by Society, 1907, Vol. XXXV)
     9, 14-15.
5.   JLC, Letterbook, 45; Spear, 243, William D. Matter, *If It Takes All Summer: The
     Battle of Spotsylvania* (Chapel Hill: The University of North Carolina Press, 1988)
     331-41; "Last Campaign of the War," *Brunswick Record*, February 5, 1904.
6.   Philip S. Wilder, ed., *General Catalogue of Bowdoin College* (Portland, Maine:
     Anthoensen Press, 1950) 115; *OR*, XL, I, 603; Survivor's Association, *History of the
     121st Pa* (Philadelphia: Burk & McFetridge, 1893) 130-31; H.N. Warren to JLC, July
     7, 1888, LC; DeLacy to JLC, n.d., LC; John W. Nesbit, *General History of Co. D 149th
     Pa. Vols.* (Oakdale Pub., 1908) 51; Thomas Chamberlain, *History of the 150th Regi-
     ment Pa Volunteers* (Philadelphia: McManus, 1905) 261; B Kevin Bennett, "Major
     General Charles Griffin: Granville's Forgotten Hero," *Newsletter of the Granville,
     Ohio Historical Society* XII, 1, Winter 1998.)
7.   JLC to John Chamberlain, Bowdoin College, December 19, 1864; Charles Griffin,
     Brig. Gen. to Gen. S. Williams, October 7, 1863, William Noble Papers, Special Col-
     lections Library, Duke; Joseph J. Bartlett to Gen. S. Williams, June 6, 1864, NA,
     endorsed by Griffin.
8.   Beauregard "Letter" 122; Roebling, 103-5; [Pierre] G.T. Beauregard, "Four Days
     Battle at Petersburg," *Battles and Leaders of the Civil War* (New York: Century,
     1884, 1888, vol. IV) 543-44; *OR*, XL, II, 157, 161, 165, 171-77,185-87, 280, 668;
     Humphreys, 222.
          Robert Tilney, *My Life in the Army* (Philadelphia: Ferris & Leach, 1912) 102-3;
     James G. Scott and Edward A. Wyatt, *Petersburg's Story* (Petersburg: 1960) 24-31;
     A. M. Judson, *History of the Eighty-third Regiment Pennsylvania Volunteers* (Erie:
     B.F.H. Lynn Publisher) 104; Richard E. Matthews, *The One Hundred Forty-ninth
     Pennsylvania Volunteer Infantry Unit in the Civil War* (Jefferson, No. Carolina: 1994)
     180; JLC, "Reminiscences of Petersburg & Appomattox," October, 1903," reprinted
     in *Bayonet Forward* (Gettysburg: Stan Clark Military Books) 46; *OR*, XL, I, 455;
     Agassiz, 166-69; Gibbs, 93-94.
          Days after the battle, Crawford would complain bitterly to Warren about Griffin's
     breach of military etiquette. Warren, commenting that June 18 had been a very
     trying day, eventually placated the disgruntled Crawford by explaining that he had
     urged Griffin to move forward with the greatest rapidity, and that he, Warren, would
     accept full blame for Griffin's transgression.
9.   JLC, "Reminiscences," see Appendix A; *OR* XL, I, 481, 490; H.N. Warren to JLC,
     July,7, 1888, LC; Gibbs, 94.

10. Anonymous, "Last Campaign of the War," *The Brunswick [Maine] Record*, February 5, 1904; Gibbs, 94; *OR* XL, II, 174; JLC, Letterbook PHS, 3; JLC, *Passing of the Armies* (New York: Bantam Edition, 1992) 93, 108; JLC, "Reminiscences" See Appendix A.

11. Gibbs, 94; H.N. Warren to JLC, July 7, 1888, LC; Horatio Warren, *Two Reunions of the 142nd Regiment, Pa. Vols* (Buffalo: The Courier Co., 1890) 34-35; Lykes, 7; JLC, "Reminiscences," 47, 49; JLC, Letterbook, 3.

12. Allan Nevins, ed. *A Diary of Battle* (New York: Harcourt, Brace & World, 1962) 363, 365, 395-99, 407; Levi W. Baker, *History of the Ninth Massachusetts Battery* (Lancaster, Ohio: Vanberg Publishing, 1996 Reprint) pp. 56-67.

    Bigelow and his 9th Massachusetts Battery are remembered for their heroic stand at Gettysburg on July 2, 1863, at the Trostle House. Chamberlain, in "The Grand Review," described Bigelow at Gettysburg with the words, "who on the exposed front fell back only with the recoil of his guns before the hordes swarming through the Peach Orchard, giving back shot, shrapnel, canister, rammer, pistol and saber, until his battery — guns, limbers, horses, men, and he himself, were a heap of mingled ruin...."

    JLC, "Reminiscences..." 47; A.P. Smith, *History of the Seventy-Sixth New York Volunteers* (Cortland, New York: 1867) 306; O.B. Curtis, *History of the 24th Michigan* (Detroit: Winn & Hammond, 1891) 262; *OR* XL, II, 177-79, 183; Robert Goldthwaite Carter, *Four Brothers in Blue* (Austin: University of Texas Press, 1978 reprint) 438-40; Edwin C. Bennett, *Musket and Sword* (Boston: Coburn Publishing, 1900) 274-79; *OR* XL, I, 457, 461, 482, 486.

13. JLC to Sarah Brastow Chamberlain, April 4, 1899, LC; JLC, "Reminiscences"; "The Last Campaign of the War," *Brunswick Times Record*, February 5, 1904; George Gordon Meade, *The Life and Letters of George Gordon Meade* (New York: Charles Scribner's Sons, 1913, Vol. II) 205-6; *OR*, XL, I, 25; Alice Trulock, *In the Hands of Providence* (Chapel Hill: University of North Carolina Press, 1992) 460-61, en. 35; Agassiz, 167-170; *OR*, XL II, 155-56; Boatner, 169.

14. JLC, "Reminiscences," See Appendix A; Beauregard, "Letter" 122-23; Beauregard, "Four" 543; "Diary of First Corps, A.N.V., while Commanded by Lt.-Gen. R.H. Anderson," *Southern Historical Society Papers* (Richmond: Rev. J. William Jones) p. 504; Calvin L. Collier, *"They'll Do To Tie To!"* (Little Rock: Pioneer Press, 1959) 195; J.F.J. Caldwell, *The History of a Brigade of South Carolinians First Known as 'Gregg's' & Subsequently as 'McGowan's Brigade* (Dayton, OH: Morningside Press, 1992 Reprint) 215; Anonymous, "Campaign."

15. Wilder, 54, 553; *Who Was Who in America* (Chicago: A.N. Marquis 1967 edition) pp. 248, 438, 587, 658-59.

16. DeLacy to JLC, n.d., LC, 5; JLC to [fragment], Chamberlain collection, n.d., Maine Historical Society; Carter, 440; John L. Parker, *History of the Twenty-Second Massachusetts Infantry* (Boston: The Regimental Association/Rand Avery Co., 1887) 472-73; H.N. Warren to JLC, July 7, 1888.

17. *OR* XL, I, 482, 488; Nevins, 384-86; JLC, "CFH" paragraph #12; L.C. Bateman, "The Hero of Gettysburg," *Lewiston Journal* 1-6 Sept. 1900; *121st Pa*, 79; DeLacy to JLC, n.d., LC; Gibbs, 205-6.

18. JLC to Sarah Chamberlain Farrington, January 29, 1882, University of Maine, Orono; see JLC, "Reminiscences" Appendix A; *Survivors 121st*, 79; Patrick DeLacy to JLC, nd, LC, 9-10; Nevins, 424-25.

19. *OR* XL, I, 473-77; A.P. Smith, *History of the 76th Regiment New York Volunteers* (Gaithersburg, MD: Van Sickle Military Books, 1988 reprint) 306-7; Rufus Dawes, *Ser-*

vice with the Sixth Wisconsin Volunteers (Dayton: Morningside, 1984) 291; O.B. Curtis, *History of the 24th Michigan of the Iron Brigade* (Detroit: Winn & Hammond, 1891); Philip Cheek & Mair Pointon, 262-63; *History of the Sauk County Riflemen: Known as Co. "A" 6th Wisconsin* (Gaithersburg, MD: Van Sickle Military Books, 1984 reprint) pp. 114-16; Wainwright, 425; Roebling, 107; DeLacy to JLC, 9; Warren, 142nd, 35-36.

20. DeLacy to JLC, n.d., LC, 5; H.N. Warren to JLC, July 7, 1888, LC; *Atlas*, plate LXIV, 1; JLC, "Reminiscences" see Appendix A.

21. JLC to Sarah Chamberlain Farrington, January 29, 1882, University of Maine, Orono; West Funk to Maine Legislature, n.d., LC; 121st, 239; Bateman, "The Hero of Gettysburg" *Lewiston Journal*, 1-6 Sept. 1900; Gibbs, 94-95; H.N. Warren to JLC, July 7, 1888, LC; DeLacy, 7.

22. Dr. George Files' Report, JLC Medical File, PHS; JLC Medical Record, Examining Surgeons Certificate, February 19, 1869, NA; George T, Little, *Genealogical and Family History of the State of Maine* (New York, Lewis Historical Publishing Co., 1909) 133.

23. West Funk to the Maine Legislature, n.d., LC; Bateman; "Campaign"; John Bigelow to JLC, April 1883, Maine Historical Society; JLC, "Reminiscences"; Nevins, 425; Chamberlin, 262-63; *121st*, 80-81; Warren to JLC, July 7, 1888, LC; DeLacy to JLC, n.d. LC; Nesbit, 34; Carter, 440, 472-73; John L. Parker, *History of the 22nd Massachusetts Infantry* (Boston: Regimental Association, 1887) 472-73; *OR*, XL, II, 180-82, 184, 188; DeLacy to JLC, n.d., LC; Matthews, 183-86; Gibbs, 94-95, 204-7; *OR*, XL, I, 477-78.

24. John Bigelow to JLC, April 27, 1883, Maine Historical Society; *Atlas*, plate XL, #1, JLC, "Reminiscences" see appendix A.

25. Thomas J. Howe, *Wasted Valor: The Petersburg Campaign June 15-18* (Lynchburg, Virginia: H.E. Howard, Inc. 1988) 119; DeLacy to JLC, n.d., LC; Edwin March to JLC, June 8, 1895, Maine Historical Society; George A. Otis, *The Medical & Surgical History of the War of the Rebellion* (Washington: GPO, 1876) II, 363; Francis Heitman, *Historical Register & Dictionary of the United States Army* (Washington: GPO, 1903) I, 371; Boatner, 668; Spear, 123; JLC, *Passing*, 266; DeLacy to JLC, n.d., LC; *OR* XL II 182, 216; H.N. Warren to JLC, July 7, 1888, LC; JLC, 265; 121st, 79-80; JLC to Fanny Chamberlain, September 17, 1862, Don Troiani Collection; Humphreys, 224; *OR* XL, I, 218.

26 For information on the Chamberlains and family, see Diane Smith, *Fanny & Joshua: The Enigmatic Lives of Frances Caroline Adams and Joshua Lawrence Chamberlain* (Gettysburg, PA: Thomas Publications, 1999); JLC to Fanny, June 18, 1864, Bowdoin College.

27. "Army Correspondence," June 20, 1864, *Boston Journal*, clipping in John Chamberlain's Diary, PHS; *OR* XL, II, 182, 216-17, 236; H. C. Henries to Messrs. Wheeler & Lynde, June 28, 1864, copy in JLC, Letterbook, PHS; Diane Smith, *Fanny and Joshua*, 367-68; DeLacy to JLC, n.d., LC; Selden Connor, Franklin Drew & Abner Shaw "In Memoriam," May 6, 1914, reprinted in *"Bayonet! Forward"* (Gettysburg: Stan Clark Military Books, 1994); "Tribute to a Maine Soldier" clipping in John Chamberlain's Diary, PHS; Chamberlain, 263-64; Grant, 223-25.

28. Lewis C. Hatch, *Maine: A History — Biographical* (New York: The American Historical Society, 1919) 354; *Report of the Adjutant General of the State of Maine, 1864-65,* (Augusta: Stevens & Sayward, 1866) Vol. I, 337, 468-69, 1128; JLC to Abner Coburn, July 21, 1863, Maine State Archives; "Dr. Morris W. Townsend," *The Daily News*, 27 Feb. 1902 [copy at Richmond Memorial Library, Batavia, New York]; Eugene A. Nash, *History of the Forty-fourth New York Volunteer Infantry* (Dayton, OH: Morningside, 1988 reprint);

Wilder, 110; JLC to Sarah Chamberlain Farrington, April 4, 1899, LC; Ellis Spear to Oliver Norton & Boyd Vincent, 1916, Clarke Historical Library, Central Michigan University; For more information on the Spear/Chamberlain relationship see *Fanny and Joshua* (Thomas Publications, 1999) and *The Civil War Recollections of Ellis Spear* (University of Maine Press, 1997).

29. Spear, xi-xiii,123; Otis, 363; William A. Frassanito, *Grant and Lee: The Virginia Campaigns, 1864-1865* (New York: Charles Scribner's Sons, 1983) 268; Bateman.

30. "U.S. General Hospital, Annapolis, Md.." clipping in John Chamberlain's Diary, PHS; Gibbs, 181, 235; Wilder, 107.

31. Otis, 363; Smith, 154-55, 168, 253, 338-40; Mary T. Clark to JLC, July 11, 1865, Adams/ Chamberlain Collection, Schlesinger Library, Radcliffe College; Smith, *Fanny and Joshua*, 154-55, 168, 253, 288, 338,-40; Heitman, 981; Transcripts of the American Medical Association, 1867, XVIII, 523; Ira M. Rutkow, *A Roster of All the Regimental Surgeons & Assistant Surgeons in the Late War & Hospital Service* (San Francisco: Norman Publishing, 1990) 203, 212; JLC to Gen. J. K. Barnes, June 30, 1865, Bernard Vanderkieft Service Record, NA; George Files, M.D., "A Review of the NA records of Gen. Joshua Chamberlain..." copy at PHS; "Infantry in Hospital, Annapolis, Md.." clipping in John Chamberlain's Diary, PHS; Sarah Brastow Chamberlain to JLC, June 23, 1864, Radcliffe College; JLC Medical Records, NA; George Adams Diary, October 29, 1864, First Parish Church, Brunswick, Maine.

Notes regarding maps

The maps included in this book began as scans from *The Official Military Atlas of the Civil War*. From that scan a black and white line drawing was created. In some cases major corrections or alterations were needed. For example, the Telegraph Road, a major route for both Confederate and Union forces moving from Spotsylvania to the North Anna, did not appear on the best *Atlas* map showing that area (plate XLV #1). In addition, some smaller roads, streams, etc, not relevant to this book were deleted. In cases where there were obvious mistakes regarding locations in archival material, an explanation is given with the map. And in cases where there is some doubt about the precise location of an event, the probable location is noted.

In order to verify or correct the *Atlas* maps, the period maps listed below from the Library of Congress collection were used.

Repository: Library of Congress Geography and Map Division, Washington, D.C.

Map of parts of Caroline, Hanover, and Henrico counties, Va., west of the Mattaponi River and the Richmond, Fredericksburg, and Potomac Railroad.
Call number: G3883.C3 186- .M2 Vault : Hotch 25
Digital ID: g3883c cwh00025 http://hdl.loc.gov/loc.gmd/g3883c.cwh00025

White House to Harrisons Landing Prepared by command of Maj. Gen. George B. McClellan U.S.A., commanding Army of the Potomac. Compilation under the direction of Brig. Gen. A. A. Humphreys, by Capt. H. L. Abbot, Top Engrs. Engraved by W. H. Dougal. 1862.
Call number: G3883.H4S5 1862 .A2 CW 594
Digital ID: g3883h cw0594000 http://hdl.loc.gov/loc.gmd/g3883h.cw0594000

Map of Spotsylvania and Caroline Counties, Virginia.
   Call number: G3883.S6 186- .M2 Vault : Hotch 62
   Digital ID: g3883s cwh00062 http://hdl.loc.gov/loc.gmd/g3883s.cwh00062

Map of Hanover County, Virginia.
   Call number: G3883.H3 186- .M2 Vault : Hotch 37
   Digital ID: g3883h cwh00037 http://hdl.loc.gov/loc.gmd/g3883h.cwh00037

Map of Spotsylvania County, Virginia.
   Call number: G3883.S6S5 186- .M2 Vault : Hotch 59
   Digital ID: g3883s cwh00059 http://hdl.loc.gov/loc.gmd/g3883s.cwh00059

Caroline County, Virginia / Eng. Office, 2d Corps, A.N.Va.
   Call number: G3883.C3 186- .C6 Vault : Hotch 24
   Digital ID: g3883c cwh00024 http://hdl.loc.gov/loc.gmd/g3883c.cwh00024

Map of Hanover County, Va.
   Call number: G3883.H3S5 186- .M22 Vault : Hotch 39
   Digital ID: g3883h cwh00039 http://hdl.loc.gov/loc.gmd/g3883h.cwh00039

Map of Prince George Co., Va. / made under the direction of A.H. Campbell, P.E. in charge of the Top.
   Dept. D.N.Va. by S.L. Sommers, asst. engr. ; app. July 18, 1864 by Albert H. Campbell..
   Call number: G3883.P65 1864 .S6 Vault : Hotch 54
   Digital ID: g3883p cwh00054 http://hdl.loc.gov/loc.gmd/g3883p.cwh00054

Map of Caroline County, Va. / from surveys under the direction of Capt. A.H. Campbell, P. Engr's &
   Chief of Top'l. Department, 1862.
   Call number: G3883.C3 1862 .C2 Vault : Hotch 23
   Digital ID: g3883c cwh00023 http://hdl.loc.gov/loc.gmd/g3883c.cwh00023

Map of King William County, Va. / surveyed & under the direction of Captain John Grant, P.A.C.S. ; A.S.
   Barrows principal assis't eng. ; made under the direction of A.H. Campbell, Capt. P.E. & Chf. Top.
   Dept., scale 1 3/5 in. to one mile or 1:40,000 ; approved by him Jan. 22nd 1863; reduced from above
   by Jed. Hotchkiss, Capt. Top. Eng. 2nd Corps, August 27th 1863, to 1/80,000 scale.
   Call number: G3883.K6 1863 .H6 Vault : Hotch 42
   Digital ID: g3883k cwh00042 http://hdl.loc.gov/loc.gmd/g3883k.cwh00042

Map of Spotsylvania County / surveyed by and under the direction of Captain John Grant P.A.C.S. ; S.T.
   Pendleton, Principal Asst. Engr.
   Call number: G3883.S6 1862 .G7 Vault : Hotch 58
   Digital ID: g3883s cwh00058 http://hdl.loc.gov/loc.gmd/g3883s.cwh00058

North Anna. [May 1864] From surveys under the direction of Bvt. Brig. Gen. N. Michler, Maj. of Engineers, by command of Bvt. Maj. Genl. A. A. Humphreys, Brig. Genl. & Chief of Engineers. Surveyed
   and drawn by Maj: J. E. Weyss, assisted by F. Theilkuhl, J. Strasser & G. Thompson. Photolith. by
   the N.Y. Lithographing, Engraving & Printing Co., Julius Bien, Supt. 1867.
   Call number: G3882.N4S5 1867 .M5 CW 590.1
   Digital ID: (copy 1) g3882n cw0590100 http://hdl.loc.gov/loc.gmd/g3882n.cw0590100

BIBLIOGRAPHY

PAPERS, ARTICLES, BOOKLETS, REPORTS:

Anderson, R. H. "Official Diary of First Corps, A.N.V." *Southern Historical Society Papers*, Richmond, VA: Rev. J. William Jones, VII.

Anonymous. "Dr. Morris W. Townsend." *The Daily News*, 27 Feb. 1902 [copy at Richmond Memorial Library, Batavia, New York].

Anonymous. "Last Campaign of the War." *Brunswick Record*, 5 Feb. 1904.

Bateman, L.C. "The Hero of Gettysburg." *Lewiston Journal*, 1-6 Sept. 1900.

Beauregard, [Pierre] G.T. "Four Days Battle at Petersburg." *Battles and Leaders of the Civil War*, New York: Century, 1884, 1888, vol. IV.

Beauregard, [Pierre] G.T. "Letter of General G.T. Beauregard to General C.M. Wilcox." Papers of the Military Historical Society of Massachusetts, vol. V.

B. Kevin Bennett. "Major General Charles Griffin: Granville's Forgotten Hero." *Newsletter of the Granville, Ohio Historical Society*, XII, 1, Winter 1998.

Chamberlain Association. "Joshua Lawrence Chamberlain; A Sketch."

Chamberlain, Joshua. "Reminiscences of Petersburg and Appomattox: October, 1903." *War Papers*, Portland, ME: Lefavor-Tower, 1908, reprinted Wilmington, NC: Broadfoot Publishing, 1992, v. III, p. 161-182.

Connor, Selden, Franklin Drew & Abner Shaw. "In Memoriam" 6 May 1914, reprinted in *"Bayonet! Forward"* Gettysburg, PA: Stan Clark Military Books, 1994.

Glenn, John F. "Brave Defense of the Cockade City." *Southern Historical Society Papers*, Richmond: VA, 1907.

Hagood, Johnson. *Memoirs of the War of the Secession*. Columbia, SC: The State Co., 1910.

Hatch, Lewis C. *Maine: A History-Biographical*. New York: The American Historical Society, 1919.

Lyman, Theodore. "Army of the Potomac, June 5-15, 1864." Papers of the Military Historical Society of Massachusetts, vol. V.

UNPUBLISHED SOURCES:

Adams, George. *George Adams Diaries*. First Parish Church, Brunswick, Maine.

Chamberlain, Joshua Lawrence. "The Charge at Fort Hell." William Henry Noble Papers, Special Collections Library, DU.

Clark, Nathan S. *Nathan S. Clark Diary*. Maine State Archives.

Livermore, William T. *Livermore Diary*. Special Collections, University of Maine at Orono.

Roebling, Washington A. "Report, May 4 to Aug. 20, 1864." Gouverneur K. Warren Papers, New York State Library.

BOOKS:

Agassiz, George R., ed. *Meade's Headquarters 1863-1865: Letters of Colonel Theodore Lyman from the Wilderness to Appomattox*. Boston, MA: The Atlantic Monthly Press, 1922.

Alexander, Edward Porter. *Military Memoirs of a Confederate.* New York: Charles Scribner's Sons, 1907.

Alexander, Edward Porter. *The Personal Recollections of General Edward Porter Alexander.* Chapel Hill, NC: University of North Carolina Press, 1989.

Badeau, Adam. *Military History of Ulysses S. Grant.* New York: C. Appleton & Co., 1885, II.

Baker, Levi W. *History of the Ninth Massachusetts Battery.* Lancaster, OH: Vanberg Publishing, 1996 Reprint.

Bennett, Edwin C. *Musket and Sword.* Boston, MA: Coburn Publishing, 1900.

Boatner, Mark M. *The Civil War Dictionary.* New York: Vintage Books, 1991.

Brock, R.A. *Southern Historical Society Papers.* Richmond, VA: 1907, vol. XXXV.

Brooks, Noah. *Washington D.C., in Lincoln's Time.* Athens, GA: The University of Georgia Press, 1989.

Buell, August. "The Cannoneer." Washington, DC: *The National Tribune,* 1890.

Caldwell, J.F.J. *The History of a Brigade of South Carolinians First Known as 'Gregg's' & Subsequently as 'McGowan's' Brigade.* Dayton, OH: Morningside Press, 1992.

Carter, Robert Goldthwaite. *Four Brothers in Blue.* Austin, TX: University of Texas Press, 1978 reprint.

Chamberlain, Joshua Lawrence. *"Bayonet! Forward"* Gettysburg, PA: Stan Clark Military Books, 1994.

Chamberlain, Joshua Lawrence. *Passing of the Armies.* New York: Bantam, 1993.

Chamberlain, Thomas. *History of the One Hundred and Fiftieth Regiment Pennsylvania Volunteers, Second Regiment, Bucktail Brigade.* Baltimore, MD: Butternut & Blue reprint, 1986.

Cheek, Philip & Mair Pointon, 262-63; *History of the Sauk County Riflemen: Known as Co. "A" 6th Wisconsin.* Gaithersburg, MD: Van Sickle Military Books, 1984 reprint.

Collier, Calvin L. "They'll Do To Tie To!" Little Rock, AR: Pioneer Press, 1959.

Curtis, O.B. *History of the Twenty-fourth Michigan of the Iron Brigade.* Detroit, MI: Winn & Hammond, 1891.

Davis, Charles E. *Three Years in the Army: The Story of the Thirteenth Massachusetts Volunteers.* Boston, MA: Estes and Lauriat, 1894.

Davis, George B. *Atlas to Accompany the Official Records of the Union and Confederate Armies.* New York: Gramercy Books, 1983 reprint.

Davis, George B. *The War of the Rebellion: A Compilation of the Official Records of the Union and Confederate Armies.* Washington, DC: GPO, 1892.

Dawes, Rufus. *Service with the Sixth Wisconsin Volunteers.* Dayton, OH: Morningside, 1984.

Dowdey, Clifford. *The Wartime Papers of R.E. Lee.* New York: Bramhall House, 1961.

Frassanito, William A. *Grant & Lee: The Virginia Campaigns.* New York: Scribner's Sons, 1983.

Gerrish, Theodore. *Army Life: A Private's Reminiscences of the War.* Portland, ME: Hoyt, Fogg, & Donham, 1882.

Gibbs, James M. *History of the First Battalion Pennsylvania Six Months Volunteers & 187th Regiment Pennsylvania Volunteer Infantry.* Harrisburg, PA: Survivors' Association, 1905.

Grant, Ulysses S. *Personal Memoirs of U.S. Grant.* New York: Charles L. Webster & Co, 1886.

Hagood, Johnson. *Memoirs of the War of the Secession.* Columbia, SC: The State Co., 1910.

Heitman, Francis. *Historical Register & Dictionary of the United States Army.* Washington, DC: GPO, 1903, I

Hopper, George C. *First Michigan Infantry: Three Months and Three Years.* Coldwater Courier Print, 1891.

Howe, Thomas J. *Wasted Valor: The Petersburg Campaign June 15-18.* Lynchburg, VA: H.E. Howard, Inc. 1988.

Humphreys, Andrew A. *The Virginia Campaign of '64 and '65: The Army of the Potomac and the Army of the James.* New York: Charles Scribner's Sons, 1883.

Hunt, Roger D. *Brevet Brigadier Generals in Blue.* Gaithersburg, MD: Olde Soldiers Books, 1990.

Judson, A. M. *History of the Eighty-third Regiment Pennsylvania Volunteers.* Erie, PA: B.F.H. Lynn Publisher, nd.

Little, George T. *Genealogical and Family History of the State of Maine.* New York, Lewis Historical Publishing Co., 1909.

Lykes, Richard Wayne. *Campaign for Petersburg.* Washington, DC: GPO, National Park Service History Series, 1970.

Macnamara, Daniel. *The History of the Ninth Regiment Massachusetts Volunteer Infantry.* Boston, MA: E.B. Stillings, 1899

Matter, William. *If It Takes All Summer.* Chapel Hill, NC: University of North Carolina, 1988.

Matthews, Richard E. *The One Hundred Forty-ninth Pennsylvania Volunteer Infantry Unit in the Civil War.* Jefferson, NC, 1994.

Meade, George Gordon. *The Life and Letters of George Gordon Meade.* New York: Charles Scribner's Sons, 1913.

Miller, J. Michael. *The North Anna Campaign: "Even to Hell Itself."* Lynchburg, VA: H.E. Howard, 1989.

Nash, Eugene A. *History of the Forty-fourth Regiment New York Volunteer Infantry in the Civil War.* Dayton, OH: Morningside, 1988 reprint 1910 edition.

Nesbit, John W. *General History of Co. D 149th Pa. Vols.* Oakdale Pub., 1908.

Nevins, Allan. *Diary of a Battle: The Personal Journals of Colonel Charles S. Wainwright.* New York, Harcourt, Brace & World, 1962.

The One Hundred Fifty-fifth Regimental Association. *Under the Maltese Cross* (Campaigns 155th Pennsylvania Regiment). Pittsburgh, PA: The Werner Co., 1910.

Osborne, William. *The History of the Twenty-ninth Regiment of Massachusetts Volunteer Infantry.* Boston, MA: Albert J. Wright, 1877.

Otis, George A. *The Medical & Surgical History of the War of the Rebellion.* Washington, DC: GPO, 1876, II.

Owen, C.W. *The First Michigan Infantry; Three Months and Three Years.* Quincy Herald Print.

Parker, Francis J. *The Story of the 32nd Regiment Massachusetts Infantry.* Boston, MA: C.W. Alkins, 1880.

Parker, John & Robert Carter. *Four Brothers in Blue.* Austin, TX: University of Texas, 1978 reprint.

Parker, John L. *History of the Twenty-Second Massachusetts Infantry, the Second Co. Sharpshooters, and the Third Light Battery.* Boston, MA: The Regimental Association, 1887.

Phisterer, Frederick. *New York in the War of the Rebellion*. Albany, NY: J.B. Lyon Co., 3rd Edition, vol. 1 1912.

Powell, William H. *The Fifth Army Corps* (Army of the Potomac). New York: G.P. Putnam's Sons, 1896.

Report of the Adjutant General of the State of Maine for the Years 1864 and 1865. Augusta, ME: Stevens & Sayward, 1866.

Rutkow, Ira M. *A Roster of All the Regimental Surgeons & Assistant Surgeons in the Late War & Hospital Service*. San Francisco, CA: Norman Publishing, 1990.

Schaff, Morris. *The Battle of the Wilderness*. Boston, MA: Houghton Mifflin 1910.

Scott, James G. & Edward A. Wyatt. *Petersburg's Story*. Petersburg, VA: 1960.

Sifakis, Stewart. *Who Was Who in the Union*. New York: Facts on File, 1988.

Smith, A.P. *History of the Seventy-Sixth New York Volunteers*. Cortland, NY: 1867.

Smith, Diane Monroe. *Fanny & Joshua: The Enigmatic Lives of Frances Caroline Adams and Joshua Lawrence Chamberlain*. Gettysburg, PA: Thomas Publications, 1999.

Spear, Ellis. *Civil War Recollections of General Ellis Spear*. Orono, ME: University of Maine Press,1997.

Starr, Stephen Z. *The Union Cavalry in the Civil War*. Baton Rouge, LA: Louisiana State University Press, 1981.

Steere, William. *The Wilderness Campaign*. Harrisburg, PA: Stackpole, 1960.

Trulock, Alice. *In the Hands of Providence*. Chapel Hill, NC: University of North Carolina Press, 1992.

Survivors' Association. *History of the Corn Exchange Regiment 118th Pennsylvania Volunteers*. Philadelphia, PA: J.L. Smith, 1888.

Survivors Association. *History of the 121st Regiment Pennsylvania Volunteers*. Philadelphia, PA: Press of Burk & McFetridge Co., 1893.

Tilney, Robert. *My Life in the Army: Three Years and a Half with the Fifth Army Corps*. Philadelphia, PA: Ferris & Leach, 1912.

Walsh, Jack. *Medical Histories of Union Generals*. Kent, OH: Kent State University Press, 1996.

Warren, Horatio. *Two Reunions of the 142nd Regiment, Pa. Vols*. Buffalo, NY: The Courier Co., 1890.

Who Was Who in America. Chicago, IL: A.N. Marquis 1967.

Wilder, Philip S., ed. *General Catalogue of Bowdoin College*. Portland, ME: Anthoensen Press, 1950.

Wycoff, Mac. *A History of the Second South Carolina Infantry: 1861-65*. Fredericksburg, VA: Sergeant Kirkland's Museum and Historical Society, 1994.

ABOUT THE AUTHOR

Diane Monroe Smith is a native of Maine. She received her degree in Human Development, the study of human relationships, from the University of Maine. Diane is a retired social worker, currently working at the Bangor Public Library. Married to Robert E. (Ned) Smith, they have two sons, Robert and Alex.

THOMAS PUBLICATIONS publishes books about the American Colonial era, the Revolutionary War, the Civil War, and other important topics. For a complete list of titles, please visit our website at:

www.thomaspublications.com

Or write to:

THOMAS PUBLICATIONS
P.O. Box 3031
Gettysburg, Pa. 17325